GHOSTS AND LEGENDS
OF WALES

Ghosts & Legends of Wales

By J. A. Brooks

Jarrold Publishing, Norwich

I would like to thank Robin Gwyndaf, of the Welsh Folk Museum, St Fagan's (a part of the National Museum of Wales) for allowing me to use stories that he has collected. His translations have brilliantly caught the bouncing rhythms of Welsh speech, and certainly serve to enliven the text.

ISBN 0–7117–0293–4
© Jarrold Publishing 1987
Published by Jarrold Publishing, Norwich
Printed in Great Britain. 2/91

Contents

Ghosts in General

About thirty years ago, when the Gwydr Forest was newly planted above and about Betws-y-Coed, a foreman of one of the gangs working there was startled by coming across a group of his workers standing idle in the middle of one of the drives, billhooks in hands. As he approached he saw that some looked thoroughly scared, others rather sheepish. They told him an amazing story.

As they had been hacking away at the tangles of gorse and brambles at the side of the drive they were startled by a number of serpents careering out of the undergrowth towards them. They were 'hoop-snakes that moved like bicycle wheels' which had pursued them for some distance along the drive before vanishing into the forest. The foreman, never a man to mince his words, would normally have used a few choice and obscene Welsh phrases to get the men working again, but on this occasion he sensed their fear and found a different area for them to work.

A couple of weeks later the serpents were seen again in the Parc Woods. Two men of a different gang were walking along one of the drives in the High Parc when they startled a small snake sunning itself on a bank. As they approached it curled itself up, its head alongside its tail, and rotated away across the track and into thick gorse. The men hurled a few stones into the undergrowth where it had disappeared and then resumed their walk to the Forest Office where they reported what they had seen. Several more sightings of the remarkable serpents were reported during that long hot summer, though the foresters kept the story to themselves and no accounts appeared in the press.

The High Parc woods were destroyed by a terrible fire in 1938 and no serpents, other than adders and grass-snakes, have been seen there since. Possible explanations of the hoop-snakes would include a collector dumping his specimens in an out-of-the-way location that might be congenial to the snakes and relatively safe to humans (the description of the serpents could apply to the deadly sidewinder or several other snakes of the deserts). In earlier days such an experience would almost certainly have been put down to a supernatural cause – probably the evil spirit of the notorious Sir John Wynne of Llanwrst would have been blamed, for had it not been found necessary to imprison it below the torrent of Rhaidr y Wennol (the Swallow Falls) 'there to be punished, purged, spouted upon, and purified from the foul deeds done in his deeds of nature'?

GOING TO MARKET.

Ghosts generally appear when we are least expecting them. Showell Styles's account of an unnatural happening when he was alone on the saddle which separates the two summits of Glyder mountain is convincing, at least to me, because it acts as a confirmation of vaguely similar personal experiences. Although unspectacular, these occurrences lack rational explanation, and are too often pushed into a part of our consciousness which seems to will us to forget them, or to muddle them with dreams, as in dèja-vu experiences. In *The Mountains of North Wales* Styles writes:

> It was here that I saw the only ghost I have ever seen on a mountain. It was on a heatwave day, a noontide of absolute stillness when the brassy glare of the sun seemed more like Arabia Deserta than Cambria. There was not a breath of wind at 3,000 feet as I sat panting just above the saddle of Bwlch-y-Ddwy-Glyder and sweated at the mere thought of the slog up to Glyder Fawr summit. Far down the southern slope Pen-y-gwryd shimmered in the haze. I could see (I thought) a hill-walker coming up that slope, a man or woman dressed in brown. A moment afterwards I perceived that the brown shape was not only too big to be human but also moving too swiftly up the steep boulder scree. It was more like a bear − except that you can't see through bears, and I *could* see through this thing. And I could hear it. The low roaring or rushing noise it was making swelled as it surged smoothly up to the crest of the pass twenty yards below where I was sitting and vanished over the edge of the steep northern side as though it had hurled itself into infinity. I had been able to see, before it disappeared, that it was six or seven feet in diameter, a rapidly whirling mass composed of bits of dried grass. There was still not the slightest stirring of the air near me and the whole ridge appeared utterly windless.

What explanation can be given to this phenomenom? It obeys few of the criteria in Howells's *Cambrian Superstitions*, published in 1831:

> In most of the relations of Ghosts, they are supposed to be mere aerial beings without substance, who can pass through walls and other solid bodies at pleasure. We also read of ghosts striking violent blows, and that if not made way for, they overturn all impedimenta like a furious whirlwind; the usual time for their appearance is midnight, seldom before it is dark, and no ghosts can appear on Christmas Eve.
>
> If during the time of an apparition, there is a lighted candle in the room, it will burn *extremely* blue: the coming of a spirit is announced some time

'Ghosts generally appear when we are least expecting them' (*Welsh Folk Museum*)

before its appearance, by a variety of loud and dreadful noises, and is rarely visible to more than one person, although there are several in company.

. . . a ghost has not the power to speak until it has been first spoken to; so that notwithstanding the urgency of the business on which it may come, every thing must stand still till the person visited can find sufficient courage to speak to it.

The mode of addressing a ghost is by commanding it in the name of the 3 persons of the Trinity to tell you who it is and what is its business; this may be necessary to repeat three times, after which it will in a low and hollow voice, declare its satisfaction at being spoken to, and desire the party addressing it not to be afraid, for it will do him no harm. This being premised, it commonly enters into its narrative, which being completed and its requests or commands given, with injunction that they be immediately executed, it vanishes away, frequently in a flash of light. During the narration of its business, a ghost must by no means be interrupted by questions of any kind; so doing is extremely dangerous: if any doubts arise they must be stated after the spirit has done its tale. Questions respecting its state are offensive, and not often answered.

If after the first appearance, the persons employed neglect or are prevented from performing the message or business committed to them, the ghost appears continually to them, at first with a discontented, next an angry, and at length with a furious countenance; threatening to tear them in pieces if the matter is not forthwith executed. Sometimes ghosts appear and disturb a house, without deigning to give any reason for so doing: with these the shortest and only way is to exorcise and eject them. For this purpose there must be two or three clergymen, and the ceremony must be performed in Latin, a language that strikes the most audacious ghost with terror. A ghost may be laid for any term less than 100 years, but of all places the most common and what a ghost least likes, is the *Red Sea*, it being related in many instances, that ghosts have most earnestly besought the exorcists not to confine them to this space.

The Welsh have an unfair reputation for being excessively morbid; this is certainly not helped by the innumerable superstitions in the country that concern portents of death. There are few parishes in Wales that are without tales of Phantom Funerals, Corpse Candles, or, most dreaded of all, visitations from the Gwrach-y-rhibyn (the Welsh banshee, even more fearsome then the Irish variety) or the Deryn Corph (Corpse Bird) which beats its leathery wings against closed windows, a harbinger of death. Almost any unusual sound heard in the countryside signified some form of doom. A crowing hen would bring death or disaster to the house that it faced as it crowed (one can picture the ashen-faced cottager, clad in long-johns, dashing to his henhouse in the grey dawn to check that the muddled bird was not pointing its beak towards his own dwelling).

> *A whistling woman and a crowing hen*
> *Are neither good for God nor men.*

Furthermore a cock crowing at night could foretell death as would the screech of a tawny owl. However an owl hooting in the midst of a town or village meant that some maiden who dwelt there was losing her chastity.

There are even stories of vampires in South Wales. In Glamorgan there is a very old farmhouse that was occupied by tenants. Some rooms, including the guest-chamber, were filled with ancient furniture almost as old as the house itself. The story is that in the eighteenth century a very pious Dissenting minister who was preaching in the locality stayed at the house and was given the best bedroom. He was in the habit of waking early in the mornings to compose his sermons, and on this occasion settled himself in an old chair by a window to think of on this occasion settled himself in an old chair by a window to think of topics for his congregation. When he rose from the chair he found his hand had been bleeding profusely, there was a pool of blood on the floor but he had felt nothing even though there appeared to be teeth marks on the back of his hand. At breakfast he commented to his host:

'The room is handsomely furnished but I fear there is a nail in the chair by the window.'

To this the tenant replied that more than one visitor had complained of being scratched in that chair, though the injuries were normally to the palm rather than the back of the hand. Two days later the Minister awoke in the early hours with a pain in his left side – as though a dog was gnawing his flesh. He found deep wounds on his chest – bite-marks similar to those he had suffered earlier, and when he fetched his

The Swallow Falls (*National Library of Wales*)

horse from the stable he found that it too had been bitten in its neck. When his hostess remarked at his haggard looks when he met her later he said:

'Madam, you may not know it, but I believe a vampire frequents this house. The dead man who owned the furniture comes to suck the blood from intruders, even to the grey mare in your stable. And probably he is not pleasantly disposed towards ministers of the Gospels.'

The tenant of the house replied that he was right, such things had happened to two ministers before 'but not to the ministers' nags'. Marie Trevelyan concludes the story thus:

> It was supposed that a Christian minister had effectually laid the vampire, but in the year 1850 a dignitary of the Church of England had the same experience as far as his left hand and left leg were concerned. Science failed to account for these occurrences, and it was not until a year later the old vampire story was remembered. The house is still occupied by a farmer, but the outgoing tenant had a sale of all the antique furniture and effects, and nothing more was heard of the vampire.

Almost as an afterthought Trevelyan adds that she had heard of a Jacobean vampire bed in a house in Cardiff that had killed a four-month-old baby and attacked others in the household, including the child's father.

More typical of a Celtic ghost is the Gwrach-y-rhibyn. Closely resembling the Irish banshee, this only troubles long-established families with pure Welsh pedigrees. The Gwrach-y-rhibyn is a repulsive hag with long black hair, black eyes, and a swarthy complexion. Her back is crooked and her thin figure wears a trailing black cloak. Some have seen her with leathery wings which beat against closed windows at night. She appears as a portent of imminent death within the family.

You are also doomed if you catch sight of the Cŵn Annwn. Spectral black dogs are not uncommon in Britain, and in Wales they appear in a number of forms. They are said to be hounds belonging to Arawn, the king of the Underworld, and occasionally he is to be seen, an enormous black figure who rides the stormy skies urging on his terrible hounds with horn and hunting-pole. They pursue those who will die within the year, hunting their prey quietly, moving from room to room within a mansion or cottage as they track down their victim. Neither do they always hunt as a pack; just as lethal is the single dog, sometimes scarlet with its coat dripping blood but more often black, always with eyes that burn with a liquid fire. Their prey is the souls of the unbaptised and unshriven and those whose souls are not spotless enough to reach heaven yet are not so irredeemably bad that they deserve eternal hell. Instead they are doomed to the limbo of following the Cŵn Annwn 'to the end of all time. . . . The cavalcade of doomed souls included drunkards, scoffers, tricksters, attorneys, parsons' wives, and witches' (Trevelyan).

Yet another death portent that was widely believed one hundred and fifty years ago was the Canwyll Corph, or Corpse Candle. Legend takes its origins back to the days of St David in the fifth century who 'earnestly prayed that the people he loved and among whom he toiled should have some kind of warning to prepare them for death. In a vision he was told that through his intercession the Welsh would never again find themselves unprepared: for always before such an event the people in the land of Dewi Sant would be forewarned by the dim light of mysterious tapers when and where death might be expected.' Marie Trevelyan continues by writing that St David must have prayed particularly for the people of South Wales as the ghostly lights seem to occur most frequently in that part of the country. However one of the most vivid accounts of a corpse candle comes from Cardiganshire where George Borrow was told this story:

'They foreshow people's deaths, don't they?' said I.

'They do, sir; but that's not all the harm they do. They are very dangerous for anybody to meet with. If they come bump up against you when you are walking carelessly it's generally all over with you in this world. I'll give you an example: A man returning from market from Llan Eglos to Llan Curig, not far from Plynlimmon, was struck down dead as a horse not long ago by a corpse-candle. It was a rainy, windy night, and the wind and rain were blowing in his face, so that he could not see it, or get out of its way. And yet the candle was not abroad on purpose to kill the man. The business that it was about was to prognosticate the death of a woman who lived near the spot and whose husband dealt in wool – poor thing! she was dead and buried in less than a fortnight. Ah, master, I wish that corpse-candles were as few and as little dangerous as the Tylwith Teg or fairies.'

Corpse Candles foretold accidents on land or sea: they could appear singly or in numbers where a coach would overturn or a ship be

wrecked. The theory that they might be will o' the wisps was disproved, it was said, by the times that they were seen within a room and thus could not be caused by noxious gas. (However there is a modern Vortex Theory that might shed light on the phenomenon: it was expounded by G. W. Lambert in 1964 to explain the famous ghost of Martin's Tower at the Tower of London.)

Corpse Candles took many shapes and forms: occasionally a skull was seen to bear the candle; some saw in them the likeness of the person who was to die, in other cases they merely gave hints at his identity:

> . . . they vary in brilliancy and size, according to the person whose doom it is to leave the world; thus an infant's would not be larger than that of a candle, whilst a child's 'of the larger growth' is of a proportionate size; the colour is said to be a sulphurous blue, and when any one observes their approach, if they do not move aside they will be struck down by their force, as I was informed by a person living, whose father coming in contact with one, was thrown off his horse. If they are seen to stop, the corpse will do the same at the funeral; if they move aside, it will occur so at the burial; and should two candles meet, the two funerals will do the same: it is also said that if a person looks back at one after it has passed him, he will perceive the corpse and its attendants. . . .

> From W. Howells, *Cambrian Superstitions*, London, 1831.

Supernatural happenings were believed to be most likely on one of the three spirit nights (Teir nos ysprydion) of the year when the souls of the dead are permitted a brief return to earth. These are the nights of the festivals of All Saints, Christmas, and the New Year (though it was a confident belief that no evil spirits were allowed on earth on Christmas Eve). At Llantwit Major in South Glamorgan it is said that if you peer through the keyhole of the church on one of the spirit nights you will see the ghosts of those who will die within the year inside the church. The belief that white waves are the spirits of those who have drowned also comes from Glamorgan: they return to visit us as white horses at Christmas, Easter, and on All Hallows Eve.

The timing of a ghost's visit was also strictly regulated:

> The hour that Spirits came to the earth was midnight, and they remained until cock-crowing when they were obliged to depart. So strongly did the people believe in the hours of these visits, that formerly no one would stray from home later than twelve o'clock at night, nor would any one proceed on a journey until chanticleer had announced that the way was clear –

Christmas Eve, however, was an exception, for during that night no evil spirit could appear.

Rev. Elias Owen, *Welsh Folk-lore*, 1887.

Phantom funerals are another form of haunting which seem to belong particularly to Wales. Accounts of them come from all over the country – this is from Tenby:

Some years ago, the then occupier of Holloway farm had a pretty servant-girl, with whom the 'man' of the rector of Penally fell in love: he used to steal out in the night-time to visit her. Her master was much displeased, and forbad the continuance of this sly sort of wooing; but such prohibitions are not always attended to, and the lover continued to scale the wall and woo by moonlight. One night, coming home, he had passed the turn of the road leading from Holloway to Penally, when, to his astonishment, he saw a funeral coming along the road towards the church, and recognised several of his neighbours among those who carried the coffin and 'followed'. They came on noiselessly, and he stood close against the hedge to let the funeral pass; but the bearers jostled so rudely against him that they hurt and bruised him severely, not hearing his entreaties or cries. After they had passed on, he saw, to his still greater perplexity, the whole procession go over a hedge into the next field, make a detour, and return into the road farther on. Considerably 'shaken' in every way, he sought his chamber, and in the morning was so ill, from the beating he had received, that he entreated his master to come to him, which he did, but placed no faith whatever in the man's story, saying he must have been drinking and fighting, and received a sound 'drubbing'. The servant stoutly denied this, and begged that, when he was able to walk, his master would accompany him to the spot, and he would show him where the funeral passed and repassed the hedge, which might be easily seen as they had trodden down the fence foliage. His master still refused to believe him, though he named the neighbours who were present, and the exact places they occupied in the procession. When the man was able to leave his bed, the master yielded to his entreaties: yet no trace of the funeral could be found. But when the story got abroad, the old people looked grave, declaring it was a foreshadowing of death, and that within a month there would be a funeral in Penally churchyard. It was now December, and an exceedingly heavy fall of snow lay upon the ground. It froze also bitterly, and the snow drifted in such a manner that all trace of hedge enclosure was in many cases obliterated: it was a cold, sad time. Only a week or two had passed since 'the parson's man' had seen the spirit funeral, and the worthy farmer of Holloway farm lay dead in his long-loved home! There would be, certainly, every one said, a large funeral, for he was greatly respected. The clergyman heard, with much astonishment, the names of the 'bearers': they were the same who had been named by his servant as having borne the coffin the night he had been so severely buffeted! But the most extraordinary circumstance remains to be told: the night before the funeral was of such intense frost, that the snow was frozen over field and hedge-row, as hard as if they had been the queen's highway – the bearers missed the road – passed unwittingly over the hedge at the *exact spot* the servant had pointed out to his master, as that where *he* had seen the midnight funeral pass – made the same detour in the field, and returned to the high road precisely at the place he had pointed out! This singular story was corroborated by the clergyman, who always said it was one of those facts for which he could not account, but of its being a fact he was ever ready to pledge his veracity.

From *The Book of South Wales*, Mr and Mrs S. C. Hall, 1861.

The Ghosts of Gwent

The Welsh border country (or Marches) is a countryside of steep wooded hills interwoven with streams and rivers and guarded by the ruins of great castles. Surprisingly in view of their frequently sinister appearance and atmosphere, these do not always boast of an authenticated ghost. Skenfrith has the reputation of being haunted, though the ghost there may have been the invention of a wily Welshman imprisoned in the Tower of London in 1589. He wrote to Lord Burghley, Queen Elizabeth's most powerful minister, requesting permission to seek the treasure of Skenfrith Castle for the benefit of the Crown: 'The voyce of this country goeth there is a dyvill and his dam in this castel; one sets on a hogshead of gold and the other upon a hogshead of silver.' Should he be released, the Welshman continued, he would endeavour to vanquish both these supernatural guardians, 'by the grace of God and without any charge to the Quene or your lordships. If the treasure be there, I will look for something at your hands, for the countrey saith there is great treasure. No man in remembrance was ever seen to open it, and great warrs hath been at it.' It is not recorded whether this ingenious ploy worked and the Welshman gained his freedom or whether treasure was ever found there.

A more sinister haunting belonging to the Marches is the Herlethingi – the army of the undead. Stories of the Herlethingi were common in mainland Europe during the war-torn Middle Ages. This is how Walter Map, a twelfth-century English writer describes them:

Companies of these troops of night-wanderers, who are commonly called *Herlethingi*, were very well known in England even to the present day, the reign of our King Henry II, who is now reigning over us. These armies went to and fro without let or stay, hurrying hither and thither rambling about in the most mad vagrancy, all inceding in unbroken silence, and amongst the band there appeared alive many who were known to have been long since dead. This company of *Herlethingi* last espied in the Marches of Hereford and Wales in the first year of King Henry II, tramping along at high noon with carts and beasts of burden, with pack saddles and provender-baskets, with birds and dogs and a mixed multitude of men and women. Those who first caught sight of this troop by their shouting and blowing of horns and trumpets aroused the whole district, and as in the manner of those border folk, who are ever on the watch, almost instantly there assembled various bands fully equipped, and because they were unable to obtain a word in reply from this strange host they incontinently prepared to make them answer to a shower of darts and javelins, and then the troop seemed to mingle with the air and forthwith vanish away out of sight. From that day this mysterious company has never been seen by man.

Quoted in *The Natural History of the Vampire* by Anthony Masters.

Turning southwards to Monmouth, the road into town from Skenfrith is haunted by a phantom stagecoach which has a horrendous accident when it crashes into a wall near Croft-y-Bwlla. It is only seen on dark stormy nights and is one of four phantom stagecoaches which haunt the approaches to the town. In fact for its size Monmouth has more than its share of ghosts – enough, in fact, for a small book to have been written on the subject (*The Ghosts of Monmouth*, Stephen Clarke, 1965). He mentions sightings of spectral cattle, deer, donkeys, cats, dogs, and soldiers, while the peace of the night is disturbed by ghostly footsteps in a score of houses, and the sad wailing of long-since-dead babies.

Lower Bailey Pit, an unlikely name for a house, used to be the most haunted house in Monmouth. The Pit is, in fact, a reference to the swampy woodland where the old farmhouse was situated. Although the name was appropriate to the dank area it seems that it is more likely derived from the Welsh 'Cad y put' – the Pit of the Battle. In the late 1960s the farmhouse lay deserted, crumbling gently in the dampness of its setting. Even before it had been abandoned it had its ghosts – a man with a wooden leg stomped around the upper floors, yet no one ever saw him. Terrible screams occasionally came from the cellar: a maid had once been murdered on the steps down to it. About eighty years ago the lonely property was bought by a colonel who lived there with his daughter; she avoided contact with strangers because of a hideously disfigured face which had been badly scarred by an accident with an oil-lamp.

Thus after twenty or thirty years without occupation the big old house had come to have a thoroughly nasty atmosphere: it was a place to visit with bravado after a session in the pub. Thus three young archaeologists, with their wives or girlfriends, came to the building on a dark, drizzly night. After briefly exploring the downstairs of the house (upstairs looked even more forbidding) the party settled down in a large room on the ground floor. The air seemed to turn more and more chill, there were noises from above . . . footsteps, perhaps. The

Skenfrith Castle (*National Library of Wales*)

girls wanted to leave but were made to feel foolish by the men. But then, without reason, one of them changed his mind: 'Let's go,' he said, 'I don't like the feel of this house at all.' Picking up torches, matches, cigarettes, they made their way to the door and out into the driveway. But again one of the men did the unexpected. Shining his torch on the third-storey windows he said with almost unnatural emphasis 'If there's anything in this house, it's up there', and without heeding the objections of the others turned back to the derelict house. Another of the men chased after him but was handicapped by the lack of a light and only caught him up in the hallway. 'Hang on,' he said, 'wait for the others.' But his companion, David, was already on his way upstairs: 'It's my father,' he said in a strange, emotion-laden voice, and continued climbing the stairs. By this time two more male members of the group were on the first-floor landing while the last one had just entered the house. It was his panic-stricken voice that caused them to pause: 'It's coming after me', he shouted, 'shine a torch at it.' He scrambled up the dusty, mouldering stairs as fast as he could; none of

the others could see the object that had so frightened him, yet the dust was moving on the stairs, the wooden treads bending under an invisible weight, and the sound of heavy footsteps approached. . . . The party fled up the final flight to find David in a state of hysteria, transfixed by something that only his gaze could see. The feeling of evil was an ever-increasing presence in the room, threatening all of them. Then someone was inspired: 'Let's sing, come on.' The voices were hoarse yet shrill as they started on *Bread of Heaven* but slowly they grew in confidence and the evil ebbed out of the room. David always maintained that it *was* his father that he had seen at the farmhouse even though he had been a baby when his father had died. A few years later the farmhouse was destroyed by fire and the site bought by a London property company. They put up the present building on the site, but not before there had been endless trouble in building a floor over the cellar, the scene of murder so many years before.

Down the Wye, now, to the lovely ruins of the abbey at Tintern, in the setting that inspired Wordsworth. A man and his wife on a cycling holiday visited the ruins one moonlit evening, about ninety years ago.

Left: 'The lovely ruins of the abbey at Tintern' (*National Library of Wales*)

The lady had psychic powers and was not frightened or particularly surprised when her right hand seemed suddenly to have a will of its own. It rapped several times on her knee with some force. Calmly she asked that if someone had a message for her it should be more gentle, and that it should communicate in the usual manner, that is one tap for 'no', three taps for 'yes'. Thus messages could be understood by the long-winded method of going through all the alphabet until three taps were felt. After a considerable time the lady and her husband understood the ghost's predicament. He was the shade of a Saxon soldier who had died near by and been buried without a prayer being said over his body. Unless two Masses were said in his name his spirit would continue restless. When they promised that this would be done the unseen ghost left them. The Masses were duly said and the incident was forgotten until some years later when the couple attended a seance. The code was rapped on the table: 'Very many thanks for the Masses said', and two ladies present swore that they saw the misty outline of a bearded figure behind the lady who had visited Tintern on a moonlit evening long ago.

Llanvihangel Court, four miles north of Abergavenny on the road to Hereford, is haunted by both a White Lady and a little green man. The White Lady always walks at midnight, from the hallway of the Court to the Lady Wood close by, where she vanishes. On the slopes of Mynydd Maen which overlooks Pontypool from the west, there is said to be a spring from which comes the sound of organ music, so sweet that it entices children within the hill itself. They are never seen again. Room 3 at the Cross Keys Inn at Usk harbours a ghost, possibly that of a young servant-girl who committed suicide here long ago or it may be the spirit of a monk martyred near by in the reign of Elizabeth I. Newport Castle has the ghost of a giant, a fierce figure who vanishes as quickly as you can focus your eyes upon him. He is supposed to be the Norman founder of the castle, Robert FitzHamon.

In and Around Cardiff

Despite its urban setting, Caerphilly is one of the most impressive of British castles — the second largest in Europe. In the past it was often troubled by a Gwrach-y-rhibyn, in this case a Green Lady, who would flit from turret to turret so fearlessly that on one occasion some of the town boys almost caught her. Unlike the forbidding banshee-like fellow members of her ilk she seems rather to have enjoyed herself 'sporting in the wood-green wild'. Not unexpectedly, there are also stories of ghostly soldiers patrolling the battlements, while the *South Wales Echo* reported in 1984 that the security men there particularly dislike the flag tower — 'None of them like going up there because they say they can smell perfume and no woman goes up there so it couldn't be lingering from any recent visitor.'

In contrast to Caerphilly, Castell Coch is the complete fairytale castle, with turrets that any distressed damsel would be proud to wave from. It has a wonderful hillside situation and when the Marquess of Bute finished his remarkable nineteenth-century restoration of the ancient castle he planted a vineyard on the steep, south-facing slopes. Naturally such a place has its ghosts.

The castle was a crumbling ruin for two centuries before its restoration, and its dereliction led to tragedy when the young son of Dame Griffiths fell into a bottomless pool of dark water within the precincts and was never seen again. His mother was inconsolable and soon died of her grief, but her ghost restlessly continued to seek her son, wandering about the castle and its surrounding woods. It was probably after this tragic episode that a lady of good family refurbished four or five rooms of the old castle and came to live there, cared for by two elderly servants, a man and his wife. They were disturbed on several occasions by inexplicable noises which were explained away by the activities of rats or jackdaws. Then one night the lady woke suddenly to find an old gentleman, splendidly dressed in the Cavalier style, staring at her. His pale, lined features wore an expression of unutterable grief and when she made to get up he vanished through a door hidden by shadow. When she attempted to open the door to follow him she found it securely locked and bolted. This same gentleman was encountered on several more occasions; he usually disappeared by passing through stonework or locked doors. A local legend explained the circumstance by reference to the owner of the castle in the Civil War. He had hidden a vast treasure in a secret underground passage that led to Cardiff Castle, but had then been killed when the barrel of a cannon disintegrated. Although the lady learned to live with the ghostly Cavalier, he so terrified the two old retainers that she eventually gave up her home at Coch Castle.

A further legend of the treasure of Castell Coch was given in an early guidebook to the district written in 1858 by Robert Drane, a Cardiff chemist. Tradition has it that the treasure belonged to the fierce Welsh soldier, Ivor Bach, who had two of his men bewitched into eagles so that they might always guard the hoard. This is Drane's account of the discovery of the treasure:

Some years afterwards *(the lady of noble birth leaving the castle)*, a party of stout-hearted gentlemen resolved to explore this subterraneous passage, wherever it might lead to. So, provided with torches and pickaxes, they set out on their expedition. On and on they went, and at last, shining through the darkness, they saw four bright red lights: very bright and very red they were. Nothing daunted they advanced, and presently found that the four red lights were the eyes of two huge eagles, who were composedly perched on an *IRON CHEST*. Now here was confirmation of the legend of Coch Castle! They walked bravely forward, when suddenly the eagles sprang upon them with claw and beak; and very glad they were to make good their retreat, while the royal birds flew back to the chest. But the men were persevering fellows, and the following day returned armed with pistols and eight good bullets, and when they came within proper distance of the eagles they fired, but with no effect; their enemies flew screaming towards them, beat out their torches with their wings, and sent the invaders back crest-fallen. They then cast some silver bullets, and got them duly blessed, and even persuaded a minister with his Holy Book to companion them. Again they saw the four red lights – an exorcism was read, which the eagles did not heed – the charmed bullets were fired with no better result than those of lead – a third assault was made by the eagles upon the disturbers of their watch and attackers of their ward, the enraged birds punishing them more severely than on either of their former visits. It is believed that the eagles are still there, though no one is bold enough to disturb them.

The fortune of the city of Cardiff in the nineteenth century owed much to the foresight of the second Marquess of Bute who gambled with his wealth in creating the docks which exported the steam coal of Wales to all corners of the world. He began the restoration of Cardiff

'Castell Coch is the complete fairytale castle....'

Castle but died there in 1848, collapsing in his dressing room. His son continued the restoration, engaging the architect William Burges in 1861 to make the flamboyant palace that we see today, a colourful mixture of Classical Greek, Arabian, and Gothic styles. Fortunately the core of the castle, the twelfth-century Norman keep that occupies the site of Roman fortification, was kept intact. It was in the wooden predecessor to the stone keep that William the Conqueror's eldest son, having been blinded by his captors, was imprisoned for twenty-eight years. In 1158 the same Ivor Bach (or Ivan the Mountaineer, as he was also named) that hid his treasure at Castle Coch, took the castle for the Welsh, capturing the Earl of Gloucester and his family and holding them for ransom. The Bute family left the castle in 1947 and it is now cared for by the City of Cardiff.

After the violence of its history it is not surprising that the castle is haunted, yet it seems that the best-known ghost here is not the shade of a soldier cut down in battle but that of the second Marquess. He is said to appear by walking through the fireplace of the Library, leaves this room by passing through a six-feet-thick wall into a corridor, then through the wall of the Chapel (built by his son to his memory) into the room in which he died. The main dining-hall of the castle is also very disturbed (this is not the medieval banqueting-hall in the cellar). At precisely 3.45 a.m. heavy doors open and shut by themselves and the lights flash on and off inexplicably. Until 1984 the custodian's flat occupied part of this area: it has since been moved to another part of the building. A 'faceless vision in flowing greyish-white skirts' has also been seen here and in a stockroom close by, where she is apt to mischievously disarrange things. Apparently she answers to the name Sarah, for when she is admonished with this name the bother ceases.

It may be Sarah who haunts the bridge over the River Taff close by: certainly it is another Grey Lady who waves at the castle, some say to attract the attention of Duke Robert of Normandy who was a prisoner here for so long. Her efforts would have been fruitless as he had already been blinded. In response to a series on the ghosts of Cardiff in the local paper in 1984, a reader reported seeing a man eleven feet tall in the castle grounds, wearing a helmet of dullish metal. A phantom coach also haunted the precincts of the castle, arriving in the forecourt when a member of the Bute family was about to die (it was also seen at one of their homes in Scotland).

The National Museum of Wales in Cathays Park is another famous

John Crichton Stuart, second Marquess of Bute (*National Library of Wales*)

building in the centre of Cardiff which has a ghost. It is generally supposed to be that of its architect, Dunbar Smith, who seems to have been annoyed when his ashes, which had been interred in a casket in the central block, were moved in order to make way for a new gents' toilet. Chairs are moved by unseen hands in the middle of the night and deliberately placed to trip patrolling warders.

The *South Wales Echo* of 14 October 1986 reported on a series of strange happenings that had occurred at the offices of the Automobile Association in Cathedral Road. Affectionately called 'Alice' by some of the staff, the ghost is a young lady wearing a shabby dress. Her hair is parted in the middle and drawn into a tight, old-fashioned bun at the back. Opinion is divided on whether she is benevolent or brings ill-will: some say simply that she smiles sweetly before fading away, others complain that her smile is sinister, 'perfectly horrible, showing all her teeth, rather frightening'; and the appearance is accompanied by an evil smell. Best quote came from the acting manager of the office: 'I can assure you there's nothing in it. No *substance* at all. . . '.

Also at the same address are: the ghost of a white nun; a poltergeist; and a white cat that has the ability to pass through closed doors.

Undoubtedly the most unpleasant of Cardiff's ghosts was the afanc or water-monster that lived in the whirlpool on the River Taff. Progress has done away both with the whirlpool and the afanc, fortunately perhaps, as the monster used to gorge itself on unfortunates who were swept into the whirlpool. If a body came to the surface after having been sucked below the swirling water it was thought the victim must have been a righteous man, otherwise the afanc would have claimed him. There was also a beautiful woman at the whirlpool who tempted people bathing there. If they succumbed to her charms they were whisked off 'to the mouth of perdition, where Satan waits for the souls who are beguiled by the lovely lady'. Similar 'sea-witch' stories are told of the whirlpool at Pontypridd, and the Black Pool at Cefn, Merthyr Tydfil, where she would lure the unwary to suicide.

Tongwynlais is on the northern edge of the city close to the motorway. In 1974 there were newspaper reports of a White Lady spectre in a council house at Pantgwynlais. It was pointed out that the house stood on a part of the Greenmeadow demesne, once the property of Wyndham Lewis who became Member of Parliament for Cardiff in 1820. His widow married Disraeli eighteen months after Lewis's death, and tradition has it that he proposed to her at Greenmeadow. Today there are few reminders of the romantic mansion that once stood here, but perhaps one of the many ghosts that haunted it lingers in the locality. In Roger Brown's collection *Turn of the Century Ton* he mentions three ghosts that used to frequent Greenmeadow − the first of these seems to tie in most closely with the council-house haunting.

Kate, a maidservant at the mansion in the 1840s, became deeply involved with Magpie (he wore black jacket and breeches with a white waistcoat), a tinker belonging to a tribe that frequently made their camp at Tongwynlais. He wove such a spell on her that, on his orders, she stole silver from the household which he sold. Kate was suspected of the crime, and when confronted, confessed, expecting the Lewis family to support her pleas for mercy. They chose to ignore her and she was duly hung at a scaffold close to the Gabalfa interchange, but before her execution she railed against the injustice of the sentence, and cursed Greenmeadow and the Lewises, saying that within a hundred years the house would be no more − a prophecy that proved correct. Other Greenmeadow ghosts were a tall, red-haired man who was seen leaning on his sword at a window in the Oak Room. Suddenly he dropped to his knees as if to pray and vanished. The Green Man was believed to be a servant of the family who appeared in his livery, while an unpleasant phantom hunchback lurked in a cellar. The following incident, told in a letter of 1878, also took place in the Oak Room. The lady was staying at Greenmeadow with her sister who was taken ill. At three o'clock in the morning:

> ...the door opened and 'a face with a large prominent nose and a shock of rather white hair' peered in. Then entered 'a small old man clad in a green coat and white knee breeches' with silver buttons on the coat and much lace hanging from the wrist. A silver rapier hung from a red sash at his side. For a moment he stood still and passed his hands across his eyes in a perplexed manner. The figure ignored her challenge to identify himself and commenced tapping the walls of the room near the door, moving backward and forward as he did so. 'Suddenly he threw up his arm with a gesture of great despair', and vanished.

Roger Brown adds that a Captain Mostyn had a comparable experience in the same room.

The wealth and fame of Cardiff is based on the city's position on the Bristol Channel. Many 'fringe industries' connected with the sea were spawned by the port. There were wizards and 'cunning women' who sold fair winds to captains. Modryb Sina (Aunt Sina) was one of these

'Their voyage proved to be disastrous....'

latter magicians: she frequented Lavernock, Cadoxton, and Sully in the eighteenth century.

All over Britain ghost stories exist that were invented by smugglers to deter the curious from investigating unexplained lights and noises too closely. On of Glamorgan's best legends probably had its origins in this way – it concerns the old manor house at Sully, a village notorious for its smugglers. When the old house was eventually pulled down the well was found to have a false bottom; below this was a chamber large enough to turn a horse and cart. A more sinister discovery was made below the paved floor of the old stables: here they found the doubled-up skeleton of a woman, giving confirmation to the story of the Captain's Wife.

This version of the story appeared in 1913 in *Annals of South Glamorgan*:

There was another discovery made near this old well, which gave colour to a curious ghost story connected with Sully House. Years before, the house had been tenanted by a sea captain, who traded from Sully to foreign parts in his own vessel. On one of these occasions he was accompanied by his wife. During the voyage the wife died, and the captain knowing the sailors' superstition about a corpse on board ship, doubled up the body, and put it in a lead-lined box. As soon as he returned to Sully, he brought the box to land, and placed it in the cellar of the house. Pending the ordering of the coffin, the captain took the box into the wood at the back of the house and buried it there *pro tem*. As soon as the coffin was ready, it was carried, with the help of another man, into the wood, for the purpose of transferring the woman's remains into its proper receptacle, but the box containing the body could not be found, nor was it ever found. The supposition was that some one had witnessed the burial, and supposing that the box contained treasure, it was unearthed and with its contents carried away. The ghost of the poor lady was said to walk, dressed sometimes in black sometimes in white satin, between the house and the wood, looking for her coffin. So firmly was this apparition believed in that an old resident in the manor house was one morning awoke very early by one of her maids, who told her mistress that she must leave her that day, as she had been so disturbed in the night by the ghost of a lady, dressed in white satin, standing by her bedside, that she could not sleep another night in the house. Now comes the curious part. Repairs were being done a few years ago to the stables belonging to the old house, when, on the removal of the stone flaggings of the stable yard, the doubled up skeleton of a woman was found underneath.

It was here that the body of the poor woman had been deposited, the thief disposing of the box for the sake of its leaden lining.

After this, so the story has it, the poor sea-captain went crazy when he was unable to find the body of his beloved wife.

A more romantic version of the tale appeared in the *Penarth Times* in 1925. In the latter years of the eighteenth century Henry Winstanley, a sea-captain, fell in love with a lovely girl from Bristol. Although she loved the captain, her father did not approve of him, and when Winstanley was away on a lengthy voyage he married her off to a wealthy bachelor, recently retired from the Indian Army, Colonel Rhys. They lived at Old Sully House, the young woman deeply unhappy, pining after her lost love. At last Winstanley tracked her down, and they made plans to leave together in the captain's ship. He brought his ship to Sully and rowed to the beach by the House. The prearranged signal was that he should blow three times on the bosun's whistle, and at this sound his lover appeared on the lawn waving a white handkerchief. But it seems that the Colonel was not unaware of the intrigue, and with sword drawn he rushed out to intercept Winstanley. In the ensuing mêlée Rhys was momentarily distracted by his wife throwing a scarf on his sword and his opponent seized upon this opportunity to make the death-thrust. As he died he gasped out a curse:

> *May heaven's vengeance rest upon you for all time. May the remembrance of this day's deed never be absent from your thoughts, waking or sleeping, and as often as yon moon shines upon the scene wherever your bones may be at the time, living or dead, may your spirit be forced to return to this spot and enact again this deed.*

Winstanley hurriedly buried the body in a makeshift grave in the shrubbery then rowed back to his ship with his lover. Their voyage proved to be disastrous. When they arrived at a distant port the crew deserted. They took on a new crew but they mutinied as the ship sailed into home waters. The captain and his mistress were locked into their cabin, and off Sully Island the crew set fire to the ship and then abandoned it. Winstanley and Mrs Rhys died in the flames. Just as the murder had taken place three days before a full moon, on a clear night, so they perished at a similar time, and this is when the ghost of Mrs Rhys walks, too, dressed sometimes in black, but more often in white, at midnight on bright nights three days before the moon is full. On other occasions the night air would ring with the clash of metal as the fateful duel was re-enacted supernaturally.

Cardiff Castle

South and Mid-Glamorgan

On occasions the Cŵn Annwn were blamed for circumstances that had human causes. At Pwyllywrach Manor (Witches' Well) in Glamorgan a huntsman in charge of the kennels went on a three-day drunken orgy completely neglecting his hounds. He returned to the kennels at twilight, and as he approached he heard an unearthly howling of dogs in the sky, yet no sound came from the kennels. Then from above came the cry of the huntsman: 'Tally-ho-ho!', more of a wail than a call. Rashly, with beery bravado, the huntsman answered the call with his own: 'Tally-ho-ho-ho!'. The very next moment the pack of hounds shut up in the kennels broke out, leapt on their master, and tore him to pieces so that only his gnawed bones remained. Wise folk of the district said that this was the revenge of the Cŵn Annwn whose cry the doomed man had imitated. After the dreadful incident the kennels were pulled down, but on stormy nights the sound of the ghostly huntsman's cry was heard for years afterwards (a particularly propitious time to listen for them is at midnight on the old August Bank Holiday Monday).

A wonderful account of the singular black dog (Ci Annwn) as an omen of death comes from the collection of folk tales collected by Robin Gwyndaf and kept at the Welsh Folk Museum at St Fagans. The storyteller was Mrs Catherine Thomas who came from Nantgarw and was 88 years of age when she told Mr Gwyndaf the story in Welsh:

Well, after going to a service in chapel in Nantgarw I was taking my friend Magi Gŵl home, you see, because she was not very well and was, therefore, afraid. Suddenly she took hold of my arm very tightly saying:

'Oh dear! look at that dog! look at that dog!'

And there was nothing there. I looked at the road. 'There's no dog there', I said.

'Yes, there is', said she, 'and it is looking at me. Oh! its eyes are like two stars.'

'Go on!' I said, 'you are seeing things, girl. There's nothing at all there.'

Do you know, she was trembling all over by the time we reached her home. She was scared of the dog. I had to hold on tight to her in case she fell over a stone. I took her right up to the house, and I asked her whether she wanted me to go in with her.

'Now go into the house', I said, 'and I shall close the gate on the dog and on me.' But I saw no dog. So I turned back and sure enough I was looking

'St Donat's castle has claim to be the most famous of the haunted homes of Wales'
(*National Library of Wales*)

for it too, when I was going back, but I saw nothing. I thought it was her weakness you see.

When I arrived home my mother and father were there.

'Where have you been for so long?' asked mother.

'Well! I went all the way up to Ifor Gŵl's house with Magi. She was scared, you see. She said she could see a great black dog and that it was watching her all the time.'

'Oh dear', said my mother, 'Ci Annwn' *(a hound of the underworld).* Father and mother looked at each other.

'Where does Ifor work?' asked mother.

'In Abertridwr', said I.

'Oh dear', said father.

'Why?' said I, 'there was no dog there.

'There was to her', said Mam. 'You see, it was a sign, a sign. Oh well! A pity it wasn't Mabon's Day *(a holiday for Welsh miners)* or something like it.'

Well, next morning here comes Magi to our house.

'My mother has sent me down to tell you', she said, 'that we found grandfather dead in bed this morning.'

There you are! Mam was asking me the previous night:

'Are you sure the dog was not looking at you?'

37

'No, I didn't see it', I said.

'Oh! thanks for that.'

And they believed in it. And it was true. The old man when Magi went into the house was having supper. But the next morning they found him in bed − dead.

Mrs Thomas added that there were two antidotes to the fateful black dog: showing it a small cross could make it run away, or you could say to it in Welsh: 'The blood, the blood which flowed from Jesus' side one afternoon', in which case the dog would never come near you again.

St Athan is a village close to Rhoose airport, on the way to Llantwtit Major. Near by is the site of West Norchéte (West Orchard) Castle which is haunted by a White Lady who suffered a cruel death at the hands of her husband. West Orchard was once the home of Sir Jasper Berkerolles who married Lady de Clare, a daughter of the Norman Lord of Glamorgan. Berkerolle left his wife for several years, going to the Holy Land on Crusade. When he returned he accused his wife of being unfaithful to him; she denied this but he persisted in his accusations citing his neighbour, Sir Gilbert D'Umphreville of East Norchéte, as her lover. Sir Jasper called on his experiences with the barbarians for her terrible punishment. He had her buried up to her neck in a field close to the castle and gave strict instructions that no one should approach her until she was dead of thirst and starvation. The poor woman's sister prevailed on Sir Jasper to allow her a daily visit, though she had to promise not to take her the merest crumb of food or drop of water. The visits were made early in the mornings when the dew was heavy on the grass, and by trailing her long gown through the meadow she was able to provide enough moisture to enable the beautiful victim to survive for ten days. After her death her innocence was vindicated, and on hearing the proof of this Sir Jasper went raving mad.

As told by Marie Trevelyan the story concludes:

So late as 1863 women who went sheep-milking in the early morning declared they often saw a beautiful lady dressed in white going 'round and round' a certain spot in the field, but they could not make out why.

This would imply that it is the ghost of the sister that appears rather than that of the lady so cruelly killed.

On the outskirts of Llantwit are the remains of Boverton Castle, built on a site that was occupied successively by British, Roman, and then Norman strongholds. At the time of Richard I it belonged to the Earl of Gloucester whose young daughter Hadwisa became the bride of King Richard's infamous younger brother, Prince John. When John came to the throne he divorced Hadwisa in order to marry Isabella of Angoulême, and Hadwisa was left to the seclusion of Boverton for the rest of her life. When the castle was dismantled early in the nineteenth century the ghostly figure of a tall lady with long black hair was frequently seen. She moved slowly about the crumbling ruins in a disconsolate way – occasionally the workmen could hear her weeping. Local opinion identified her as 'Wissie', the King's wife. She was known as the Black Lady of Boverton after the mourning clothes she wore, as a mark of respect for a husband she loved in spite of the cruel way he had treated her.

Llantwit Major itself is one of the most ancient villages of Wales. There was once a tailor living here who had a cheerful and robust wife named Barbara. On her deathbed, Barbara's mother-in-law entrusted her with the duty of sharing an amount of money with the rest of the family. Instead the tailor's wife kept the money for herself, and after a little the spirit of the old lady began to take its vengeance on her. It would allow her no sleep, pinching her throughout the night until she was black and blue. Barbara became haggard and ill, and was almost relieved when the ghost actually confronted her. She was given a choice: she could either distribute the money fairly or throw it into the River Ogmore (there are many stories of people not being able to rest until they have thrown their ill-gotten gains into this river). Selfishly she chose this latter course, and was at once whisked up high into the sky, so that she could see the church loft and all the village spread out beneath her. When the time came for her to throw the money into the river, she either forgot the ghost's instructions (or more likely chose to ignore them) and threw the bag upstream rather than downstream. The ghost was furious at this and after buffetting her severely in the wind, dropped her in a whirlpool. Late in the evening the bellringers found her bruised and bedraggled on the banks of the river. She had no idea of how she had come to be there, and from that moment she had no more peace, and even her husband, a good, truthful man, was disturbed by the strange noises and happenings in the house. Again the story comes from the collection made by Marie Trevelyan at the turn of the century, and she ends by saying that there were people

'Dunraven Castle itself was haunted by a little old lady in a blue dress'
(*National Library of Wales*)

living in her time who maintained that Barbara's children were 'ghost-walked' or ghost-ridden.

Marcross church is said to have woodwork that came from a vessel from the Spanish Armada wrecked off Nash Point. Long ago it was well known that the ground around a certain large stone at Marcross was haunted by a persistent ghost, who appeared regularly on the same day, year after year. At last a villager confronted the ghost and addressed it correctly. The spirit answered:

'Since you ask me in God's name, I will tell you what I want. I am looking for the bones of my brother, and cannot rest until they are found. But I am a spirit and cannot dig. Will you help me?'

The villager consented to this and dug all night long, watched by the ghost. At last bones were found and identified by the spirit as being those of his brother. They were re-interred in the churchyard, upon which the ghost said:

'He was a good man and brave, and fought valiantly for his Queen and country against the Spanish Armada.'

Then the ghost disappeared, never to be seen again.

Close by, St Donat's Castle has claim to be the most famous of the haunted houses of Wales. 'Here, for 700 years, from William Rufus to George II, ruled the Stradlings – Knights, adventurers, poets, wreckers, and travellers, a family whose every generation brought a legend, and their motto the simple and all-embracing "Duw a digon" (God and enough)' – *Western Mail*, 18 October 1937.

The castle that we see today dates from the fourteenth century. It is now used by the Atlantic College, having been sympathetically restored by the American newspaper magnate, William Randolph Hearst, who bought it in 1925 and frequently lived there with the filmstar Marion Davies. A previous owner had found the various ghosts so troublesome that he had been forced to have the castle exorcised. These events (as told to Lord Halifax who used them in his *Ghost Book*) probably took place in the early years of this century.

For some time the inhabitants of St Donat's Castle had been greatly alarmed by a variety of ghostly phenomena which appeared by day as well as by night. The materialisations which occurred scared not only the servants and the children of the house, but also the owner and his wife. The situation at length became so intolerable that the owner, a retired naval officer, decided to let or sell the place, which accordingly was advertised in *Country Life*

At this juncture, however, he happened to hear of the fame of Mr X— as an exorcist. Mr X— is a remarkable man, born in one of the Dominions, who at the age of fourteen discovered that he possessed extraordinary powers of healing. His record of cases is amazing. He devotes his life to healing the sick and to casting out evil spirits from individuals and from haunted houses.

Informed of Mr X—'s gifts, the owner of St Donat's wrote to him and invited him to pay a visit to the Castle and investigate the phenomena which were giving such trouble. Mr X— consented, and in due course arrived. He found that the principal manifestations were as follows:

1. A panther was repeatedly seen by the household in the corridors.
2. A bright light appeared nightly in one of the bedrooms, having the semblance of a large, glaring eye.
3. A hag of horrible appearance was seen in the armoury.
4. The piano, even when closed, was played by invisible hands.

Having received this account of the manifestations, Mr X— retired to the bedroom, in which the light had been reported, to pray and grapple with the Powers of Darkness. He requested the owner of the house to sit meanwhile in the hall, with the front door wide open, while the process of exorcism went on. After a while, as though to mark Mr X—'s triumph over the evil forces of the place, a great gust of wind suddenly blew out from the

room where he was praying, swept down the main staircase and all but carried the owner of the Castle into the garden.

From that day and hour the ghostly disturbances completely ceased. All was peaceful in the Castle, which is no longer to be let or sold.

Strangely the catalogue of ghosts mentioned above leaves out two of the most famous figures who haunted St Donat's, but this may be because both of them were connected specifically with the Stradling family. Lady Anne Stradling used to haunt the Long Gallery, eternally awaiting her husband's return from the Holy Land (he failed to return because he was killed in a duel in Italy that he had been obliged to fight in order to save his honour). She would appear in a long silk dress, her feet sounding loudly on the oak boards, and this would bode ill for some member of the Stradling family, for disaster invariably followed. (The American writer Wirt Sykes says that Lady Stradling was killed by members of her family 'in those wicked old times when families did not always dwell in peace together'). Just to make certain that the family understood the message the banshee-like Gwrach-y-rhibyn also used to swoop through the village and around the estate – the evil hag was supposed to have been seen on the night of the death of the last of the Stradlings in the eighteenth century, with her pack of black hounds with their red eyes and terrible fangs. Invariably this set all of the dogs (and even the foxes) in the neighbourhood barking.

The last of the Stradlings was Sir Thomas, who, although the youngest son, inherited the St Donat's estate as a wild young man and in 1738 left Wales for the Grand Tour accompanied by his disreputable university friend, Sir John Tyrrwhitt. They had made a pact with each other that whoever should die first should leave his fortune to the other. Sir Thomas mysteriously died in France in September of that year, possibly in a duel with Tyrrwhitt. When he was brought back to St Donat's to lie in state in the Great Hall the candles that were burning around the coffin set fire to the funeral decorations, and much damage was done to the fabric of the castle. Also five generations of family portraits were destroyed. Since Sir Thomas died young there was no direct heir, and a long dispute followed between various members of the family (plus the Tyrrwhitts) over the inheritance. A final variation on this theme comes from the pre-war article on the Stradlings in the *Western Mail* already quoted above:

Once a year Mallt-y-nos, Poor Matilda of the Night, comes in trailing a dark-blue gown with spectral dogs howling round her hunting for the soul of Colyn Dolphyn, a Breton pirate, whose effigy for many years was burnt at Llantwit. People say that for hundreds of years this Norman lady wandered through the castle, foretelling mishaps to the family, and some even say that on stormy nights she can be seen riding the heavens with her ghostly hounds baying and crying.

In the case of Colyn Dolphyn too there are alternative versions of the myth. In 1449 Henry, the son of Edward Stradling was kidnapped by the Breton pirate while sailing from Somerset. He was only released after the payment of a large ransom. After his father died four years later Henry built a watchtower and posted men in it day and night to look for the pirate. Legend has it that eventually Colyn was lured on to the rocks by a false light, captured, and then buried up to his neck in sand in Tresillian Cave to be drowned by the incoming tide. This echoes the story of Peter the Pirate, who was buried in the same place 'by glad landsmen, and on stormy nights at sea he can be heard tossing and turning in his rocky bed'. As a postscript the *Western Mail* adds that you will never see a snake on the Stradling estate, as one of the family imported some Irish earth!

Little more than five miles up the coast from St Donat's is Dunraven Castle, the seat of the Vaughans, and, later, the Wyndhams, Earls of Dunraven. The 'wrecker lord', Thomas Vaughan, was ruthless in luring ships on to this dangerous coast where they could easily become embayed by a south westerly wind. Many came to grief on Southerndown Beach where he himself cared for a light placed in an old ivy-covered tower. He also tied lamps to the backs of sheep and had them graze on the cliff-tops at night. Neither could the shipwrecked sailors expect mercy from Vaughan and his men: he cruelly set upon the few who survived the breakers to crawl up the beach, tearing from the corpses any articles of value before rolling them down to an ebbing tide.

One foggy night he was called to the beach to witness the wreck of a particularly fine prize. His men were clustered around a body clad in finery and richly bejewelled. His chief henchman, Matt of the Iron Hand (he had lost a hand as a punishment when he had been convicted of piracy by Vaughan, the local magistrate) drew his attention to a hand that he had severed from a corpse on the beach. From the ring it wore he realised with horror that it was the hand of his own son, who returning that night from a long voyage had fallen a victim to the

'The "wrecker lord", Thomas Vaughan, was ruthless in luring ships on to this dangerous coast' (*National Library of Wales*)

greed and savagery of his father. Matt had taken revenge for the loss of his hand. From that time the Earl fell into melancholy and died in alcoholic madness, often roaming the beach where his son died, and on the anniversary of his death, or before a wreck, he may be seen in a long flowing cloak, moaning and crying, on the cliffs and beach of Southerndown.

Dunraven Castle itself was haunted by a little old lady in a blue dress who left behind her the smell of mimosa. The castle was demolished after the Second World War.

Penllyn Castle, just to the north of Cowbridge, used to be surrounded by dense woodland which was the haunt of dragons, or winged serpents. This was believed as recently as the latter years of the last century. They were very beautiful 'and looked as if they were covered with jewels of all sorts. Some of them had crests sparkling with all the colours of the rainbow.' Unfortunately they were as bad as foxes for poultry and so were eventually hunted to extinction. Penmark, on the opposite side of Cowbridge also had its dragons in the woods near Porthkerry Park. A lady there told Marie Trevelyan that she had seen the skin and feathers of a dragon that had attacked her uncle, beating his head with its wings. It was as wicked as any fox in the nearby farmyards and coverts, but was said to guard treasure that had been 'hidden away by someone before going to the great Battle of St Fagan's when the river ran red with blood'. The Welsh dragon is usually smaller than its English counterpart, and more beautiful, with characteristically bird-like features. They are also gregarious rather than solitary creatures, and the Welsh regard them as predatory nuisances rather than as monsters which menace a neighbourhood.

An old woman who was thought to be a witch used to live on the edge of the lonely marshes which fringe the coast to the north of Porthcawl. She was supposed to take the form of a grey goose occasionally and take to the wing, and thus disturbed the duck-shooters of the marshes, who swore that they always had a bad day when the grey goose appeared. Kenfig Pool is at the centre of this marshland and is a suitable place to support a handful of legends. The local chieftain of this district once wronged his Prince who cursed him on his deathbed. Soon afterwards he and his supporters heard a voice from the sky: 'Dial a ddaw! Dial a ddaw!' (Vengeance is coming!), and this sound continued each night until the chieftain consulted a bard as to its meaning. The bard told him of the Prince's curse which was derided by the chieftain who called for a feast instead at his village.

This was well under way when the cry was heard for the final time, and almost immediately afterwards a great flood inundated the village to form Kenfig Pool. An account of 1697 supports this legend:

. . . a borough town sometime of good account but long since decayed by overflowing of ye sand, and by some ye ancient town sinked and became a great meare. . . .

while in 1805 it was said that the Pool came into being overnight as the result of an earthquake. Traces of masonry have been found beneath the surface of the Pool, and a further legend asserts that three 'devil's chimneys' rise from the Pool and belch smoke when great storms are due to hit the coast.

Just to the south of the Pool the lonely and sinister Sker House is haunted by a ghost with chains: a father who suspected his daughter was up to no good is supposed to have kept her in chains, which may be heard clanking as they are dragged across the floor. A phantom light hovers over Sker Rocks before storms, and a phantom shipwreck was once seen on the shore here. Sure enough the apparition foretold a real and tragic event which followed within a week.

West Glamorgan

One of the great tourist showpieces of South Wales lies on the eastern border of West Glamorgan. At Margam there are two romantic ruins at the same location. The castle, a picturesque mansion with Tudor and Gothic features (which was, nevertheless, only completed in 1840 as the family home of the Talbots who gave their name to Port Talbot) had a White Lady while more recently there have been several reports of the spectral figure of a Cistercian monk in the neighbouring ruins of the Abbey. It may be the ghost of Twm Celwydd Teg (Tom of the Fair Lies), a monk who worked at the Grange belonging to the Abbey. He had the uncanny knack of predicting the future. One day a young man about to go on a bird-nesting expedition asked him: 'Well, Tom, what lies have you got for me today?' Tom answered 'You will die three deaths before nightfall.' This the young man shrugged away for who could die three deaths in a day? But the prophecy was fulfilled, for finding a kite's nest at the top of a tall tree overhanging a river, he put his hand in the nest to take out the eggs and was bitten by a viper that the bird had left there for her chicks. As he fell from the tree he broke his neck, landed in the river and was drowned.

Aberavon was the name for Port Talbot before the arrival of heavy industry. Each year on Christmas Morning a giant salmon would make its way up the Afan River and allow itself to be handled by anyone, though if they harmed it in any way 'divine judgment would instantly overtake that person'.

A far cry, perhaps, from sacred salmon to portents of disaster in mines, yet the latter were probably the most ardently believed superstitions of the Welsh, and anyone catching sight of a dove, say, at a mine, could cause work to cease there almost immediately. Such a bird was seen hovering over a level in the remote Glyncorrwg mine in July 1902, and coming after a host of other omens, it was enough to make 300 miners refuse to work there. The *South Wales Echo* reported on 15 July 1902:

The men have been whispering their fears to each other for some time past, but the drastic action on Monday was probably the outcome of so-called evil omens which are said to have been heard in the mine. About two months ago the night-men began to tell creepy tales of the strange and supernatural happenings which took place in the colliery every night. . . . Now and then a

Margam Castle had a White Lady'

piercing cry for help would startle the men . . . and during the night shift horrid shrieks rang through the black darkness of the headings, and frightened the men nearly out of their wits. . . . There is, of course, the usual tale of the dove hovering over the mouth of the heading

Morfa Colliery was situated on the coast just to the south of Port Talbot, close to where the docks are today. On Sunday, 9 March 1890 a huge white bird was seen to settle on the winding gear. The next day there was a terrible underground explosion which killed 87 miners. It always had the reputation of being an unlucky pit, seldom without some sign or portent. There were the sounds of thunderous roof falls which never occurred, an apparition was seen in the cage, and another once jumped on the train: it was recognised as a miner who had died years before. At the coal face itself workers sometimes had the scent of a rose-garden waft over them. The *South Wales Weekly News* on 14 September 1901, listed other signs that the miners had noticed before the disaster:

The Morfa Colliery is situated near the sea, in a wild region. Shortly before the explosion at that colliery the men were disturbed by strange noises and tappings in one of the stalls. A bird had been seen, and the crows *(two of them, one flying east, the other west – particularly ominous portents)* had flown over the colliery. Two of the miners had even noticed the spirits of two men pass before them on the road as they left the colliery for their homes. . . . That there was amongst the miners at Morfa a wholesome dread of spirits and a belief in their manifestations was placed beyond doubt, for rumours of spirits and knockings were rife throughout the colliery village, and the terrible disaster, no doubt, confirmed many of them in that belief. The Celtic imagination has peopled the West with stories of signs and portents, mysterious beings, corpse candles, and death-hounds, and the Cornish miner is perhaps far more superstitious than the small section of Welsh colliers who repeat these reports of black crows and strange tappings and warnings of disaster.

In the nineteenth century Swansea was one of Britain's wealthiest towns, its fortune based on anthracite, tin-plate, and iron-founding. Inexorably, from about 1913, the decline of its prosperity followed on the exhaustion of the seams of anthracite. Today it is the commercial and cultural centre for the western part of South Wales. The ghost of the great Edwardian prima donna, Adelina Patti, has been known to appear in a box at the Grand Theatre, resplendent in the flamboyant costume of the period. She built a romantic Gothic castle, Craig-y-Nos, in the valleys, complete with its own bijou theatre, which is still there. Another Swansea ghost with tenuous operatic connections is Jersey Lil, not Lily Langtry, but more likely a lady of easy virtue who used to ply her trade to sailors at Jersey Marine. Another theory is that she worked at the pickle factory and died when she fell into a full pickling vat (few more horrible deaths than this are to be found in these pages).

Swansea is the gateway to the Gower, a peninsula that though small is distinctively different to the rest of South Wales, with its limestone landscape, host of ruined castles, and the contrast of its southern and northern coastlines: the former all sandy beaches and grassy cliffs, the latter a vast and lonely estuarine marsh, the haunt of seabirds and cocklers.

Pennard Burrows are hardly the most picturesque part of Gower today, covered by hundreds of caravans which look inland towards the ruins of Pennard Castle. A famous legend tells of the 'host of dwellings' which may lie, engulfed by sand, beneath the Burrows.

The castle was once held by a fierce chieftain, who was both feared and admired for his swashbuckling adventures. His successes in battle made him famous throughout Wales, and a great prince from the north of the country persuaded him to bring his army to Gwynedd to fight on his behalf. After a successful campaign the prince asked him to name his reward. In true fairytale fashion, the chieftain of Pennard asked to marry the daughter of the prince, who was both young and beautiful, and he duly took her back to Gower. A great feast was ready for them as they arrived at the castle, and the soldiers, their families, and most of the district made merry through the night. In the small hours a sentry on the battlements heard sounds distinct from the revelry within. A small green place some distance away from the castle was lit by a strange, glorious light, and a bewitching cascade of notes seemed to come from there. He ran to fetch the warder of the castle who came, watched, and listened, and went immediately to his chieftain to tell him of the curious vision. By this time the chief was inflamed by the day's drinking, and calling for his favourite henchmen he drew his sword and led them to fight, with man or spirit.

In fact they found a party of fairy elves, dancing on a grassy knoll lit by silvery moonlight. The chieftain and his soldiers floundered amongst them, slashing at the tiny figures with their swords, yet without wounding any of them, until at last, with the drunken band almost exhausted both by their efforts and with rage, they heard a quiet voice:

'. . . thy lofty castle shall be a ruin, and thy proud township shall be no more' (Pennard Castle). (*National Library of Wales*)

'Proud chief! thou warrest against those that shall now destroy thee; thou hast wantonly spoiled and marred our innocent sport – thy lofty castle shall be a ruin, and thy proud township shall be no more.' And with a wave of his wand the tiny fairy flew off into the sky, his sweet voice singing a strange song.

There must have been powerful magic in this for at once a great whirlwind came from the heavens, and with it clouds of sand which first overpowered the castle, causing its walls to crumble, and then buried all the humble dwellings of the township. Tradition had it that this sand came from Ireland, for that same night a great mountain of sand disappeared from that country, and the inhabitants of the district 'knew not where it was gone'. *(Personally I cannot believe this – Pennard is one of the few places where I have seen an adder.)*

Oxwich Bay is one of the most famous of Gower beaches, and on a summer's day it is hard to imagine this as a haunt of smugglers, as it was two centuries ago. Wynford Vaughan Thomas, in his excellent *Portrait of Gower*, quotes a strange story that happened here many years ago. It was written by the Rev. J. D. Davies, whose father was Rector of Oxwich:

> My oldest brother, now deceased, when a lad of about thirteen or fourteen years of age, had been out one evening with my father fishing in the bay. It was late when they landed, and by the time they had finished mooring the boat, it was nearly twelve o'clock. They had just gained the top of the beach, which here abuts the narrow path leading to the church, when my brother happened to look behind him, saw what he described to me, to be a white horse walking on its hind legs and proceeding leisurely along the path to the church gate; having called my father's attention to this strange spectacle, he turned round for about a minute, and watched the creature, or whatever it was, until it reached the gate, or rather the stone stile by its side, which the animal crossed, apparently without the slightest difficulty, still going on its hind legs. The uncanny thing then disappeared. The only remark my father made was, 'come along'. They were soon inside the rectory, which was only a few yards off. The strange adventure was never afterwards spoken of by my father, nor alluded to in any way. I have often been on the point of questioning him about it, but some vague feeling of undefined alarm always prevented me!

Although this tells us something of the reserve between father and son in Victorian times, there may have been another reason for the Rector's silence on the subject. Possibly he had seen the creature

'A mortal beguiled by fairies'

before, or even used him, for it was believed that clergymen and ministers of all denominations could ride the water-horse or Ceffyl-dŵr to whatever destination they required. However others tempted to mount the lovely beast would be taken high over river and mountain with the utmost ease and exhilaration, but then without warning the magical animal would turn into a swirl of mist, and the rider would fall to his destruction.

The west of Gower is a place of magic where some still believe in the Verry Volk, and the trees are bent double by the unrelenting force of the westerly winds. At the end of the peninsula is Worm's Head: at the time of Henry VIII Leland wrote of an amazing passageway which ended here, having begun at the wonderful castle of Carreg Cennen near Llandeilo.

Hole at the Point of Worme heade, but few dare enter into it, and Men fable there that a Dore withein the spatius Hole hathe be sene withe great Nayles on it: but that that is spoken of of Waters there rennynge under the Ground is more lykely.

Certainly a blow hole is still here, really spectacular in foul weather, and there is also a bone cave where the remains of mammoth, bear, and rhinoceros have been discovered.

As a baby, St Cenydd was miraculously rescued from this rocky shore by seabirds who plucked him from the wicker basket in which he had been set adrift and lowered him gently on to a grassy ledge. He had been born deformed, the offspring of an incestuous relationship between a Prince of Brittany and his daughter who had been attending King Arthur's court at Loughor. The gulls sheltered the baby with their wings until on the ninth day an angel brought a great brass bell shaped like a breast and placed it in his mouth. From this he drew nourishment, though the food it contained was itself miraculous as 'the secretions which childhood naturally discharges in its retirement, he never did, for he was fed with a most subtle food, which had no secretion'. His 'Titty Bell' later became a famous relic: it enabled St Cenydd to convert the wicked and even visit St David in Pembrokeshire (his crippled leg was temporarily healed, and he skipped off across the waves of Carmarthen Bay to see his friend).

A more tragic story of Worm's Head dates from 1712, and concerns the wrecking which many fishermen and farmers undertook in the stormy winter months when they could look for little income from their regular occupations. Kate was a very young servant-girl at the

inn at Rhossili who was often made to take out a lantern on stormy nights and walk along the shore and cliffs to tempt ships to their doom. But one Sunday the Rector preached a fierce sermon against the sin of wrecking which Kate took to heart. Soon afterwards she was sent to the Head with her lantern to lure a deeply laden merchantman which was seen at dusk to be heading towards the shore. In a terrible wind she clambered over the rocks to the cliffs, but instead of carrying the light to and fro to imitate a tacking vessel, she put a match to the pile of wood and pitch that stood ready to act as a beacon. Kate was successful in warning the ship away from the treacherous coast but she was never seen alive again. Her mutilated body was washed up a week later, and though many knew of the wreckers' anger against her, none had courage enough to make accusations against them. Many years later a man lay dying of gaol-fever in Carmarthen Prison. The Gaoler approached the Chaplain as the man appeared demented in his last agonies, seemingly wanting to confess to a crime which he nevertheless denied committing: 'Mercy, mercy lord it was not I! The girl Kate, I helped only to throw her over, it was Bill who did for her with the boathook. . . . Mercy my Lord Judge, mercy . . .'.

The view northwards from Rhossili is wonderful. The flat-topped plateau of the Downs speaks of the geological upheaval a million years ago which raised this ancient shoreline 200 feet. Just one house stands close to the sea: this is the Old Rectory which was built here to enable one Rector to serve both Llangennith and Rhossili – at great inconvenience, as only a path leads to each village. Such a location encouraged eccentricity in the incumbent and Wynford Vaughan Thomas (Portrait of Gower) mentions one who never spoke to any of his parishioners. On one occasion he met the postman in Rhossili street who offered a letter to him. The Rector ignored this, so the postman had to walk the mile out to the Old Rectory in the company of the parson, and presumably without conversation. When they arrived at the Old Rectory the Rector bowed politely, but without smiling, and took the letter from the postman.

The Old Rectory has the reputation of being well haunted, which may have been the reason for the strange behaviour of its former resident. Thomas says that he never discovered the precise nature of the haunting:

> . . . one person who stayed in the house, after the Church Authorities had wisely built a new Rectory near to Rhossili Church, told me that on a

certain winter's night 'something very unpleasant indeed comes out of the sea and comes into the house'. Another story suggests that you can suddenly walk into a cold pool of air in the corridor and hear a low voice in your ear saying, 'Why don't you turn round and look at me?' No one has ever dared.

On the dunes a phantom coach races across the sands on stormy nights drawn by four grey horses driven, it is said, by a Llanddewi man named Mansel. He is supposed to have been the first to reach the famous 'Dollar' ship when she was wrecked on this shore in the seventeenth century, and crammed his coach with Spanish golden dollars, making off before the lawful owner of the prize, the lord of the manor of Rhossili, could claim his rights (elsewhere it is claimed that Lord and Lady Rhossili sit in the coach, hurrying, perhaps, to save the treasure). Another phantom coachman haunts the Welcome to Town Inn at Llanrhidian, where he sits quietly in the front parlour, dressed in Regency clothes. Just to the east of Llanrhidian is the lost village of Llanellan − the village of the dead.

There is only a farm of this name to commemorate the place today. Long ago a ship was grounded in the estuary, and its crew and passengers made their way from the shore up the hill until they came to the village of Llanellan. Unused to receiving the survivors of shipwrecks, the villagers made them welcome. But within days it became apparent that they carried pestilence, which soon spread to the villagers, not one escaping the dreadful disease. A White Lady is supposed to haunt the ruins of the village, though no signs remain of the buildings today.

Llanellan was the estate of the Bowens, a famous Gower family, ancestors of the even-more-famous Irish writer, Elizabeth Bowen. Lieutenant-Colonel Bowen fought for Cromwell in the Civil War. However his 'careless and sensual life' found little favour in the strict order of the Parliamentarians, and at the conclusion of the war he was exiled to Ireland, leaving his wife at Llanellan. In Ireland he is said to have become 'an absolute atheist, denying Heaven or Hell, God or Devil, acknowledging only a Power, as the antient Heathens did Fate.' One night in December 1655 his wife was awoken by a great noise, 'like the sound of a whirlwind, violent beating of doors or walls, etc. Something like her husband asked her whether he might come to bed. She refused permission, and with others spent the night in prayer.'

Night after night the disturbances continued − indeed, they seemed to get worse. Terrible smells of putrefying flesh and sulphurous smoke filled the house, dimming the light of lamps and candles. People were hit so that their bodies were bruised and painful, and at length they were forced to leave the house. Colonel Bowen was sent for, but he refused to believe the stories even though his wife continued to be disturbed as before. At last the family moved to Ireland, though Mrs Bowen and most of the children soon returned to Wales, leaving her husband with the company of one son 'apparently a thorough believer in apparitions, who had seen spectral mastiffs, headless men, etc., in Warwickshire'. It seems impossible to explain the purpose of this haunting, though it was not unknown for Cromwell's propagandists to besmirch those who had come into their disfavour with the taint of the diabolic.

The South of Dyfed

This county encompasses a wonderful variety of scenery within its lengthy borders. On its seaward side, the coastline rivals that of Cornwall and Devon, while on the eastern borders the Black Mountains and the unfrequented meadows, forests and moors of Mid-Wales provide some of the most beautiful landscapes of the country. Carreg Cennen Castle is one of the most romantic landmarks of Dyfed, and the legendary passageway connecting it with Worm's Head has already been mentioned. One version of the story of Owen of the Red Hand has it that he and his 51 warriors are doomed to sleep for a thousand years in a cave close to the castle. When he awakes there will be peace throughout the world. This idyllic prospect is different from that offered by another legend which comes from Mynydd Mawr, to the west of Carreg Cennen.

> Among other traditions related by the Welsh of the valiant opposition of their ancestors to the Saxons and other enemies, is one respecting the brave and noble chieftain *Owen Lawgoch*, said to be one of the last who fought against the Saxons, and who with his gallant troops being compelled to retreat, retired to a cave on the northern side of Mynydd Mawr, near Llandeilo, Carmarthenshire, where they obtained food by foraging: every morning, it is said, the chief watered his horse at a fine spring on the summit of the mountain covered with a large stone which required gigantic strength to lift it up: after watering his horse as usual one morning, he forgot to replace the stone, and coming there the next day was terrified at the sight of a lake of water, covering a huge tract of land where the well stood. This was occasioned by his neglecting to cover the well. After relating the circumstance to his men they all laid themselves down in their armour, and were so overpowered by sleep that they never awoke, and *still* lie dormant in the bowels of the mountain, where, as the legend goes, they are to remain until awakened by the sound of a trumpet and the clang of arms on Rhywgoch, when they will resume their pristine vigour, and issuing from the cave will conquer their enemies, and drive them from their land. Llyn Llechwen (or Llyn Llech Owen, the Lake of the Red Handed Owen) is on the top of Mynydd Mawr.

As is often the case with legends, this version seems to have spawned other stories of sleeping heroes. One comes from close by in the Vale of Neath. A Welsh drover visits London for Barnet Fair, and on his way home rests for a while on London Bridge. He is approached by a

stranger who comments on the stick he holds, saying that it must come from a place where there is a hoard of gold and silver to be found. He asks the drover to take him to the tree he cut the stick from, promising that if he does so he will earn himself a fortune.

They arrive back in South Wales. The stranger tells the drover that he has seen this spot in a dream and shows him where to dig. He comes across a broad flat stone, which when raised reveals broken steps leading to a long corridor. In the middle of this passageway hangs a bell, suspended from the ceiling. The stranger warns him never to touch this: the consequences would be dire. At last a vast cavern is reached filled with sleeping warriors, who lie with shields and swords ready beside them. At the centre are twelve knights guarding King Arthur himself. The stranger says that they are waiting for the Black and the Golden Eagles to go to war. When this happens the clamour of eagle warfare would be so loud that it would make the earth tremble, and thus cause the bell to ring. Then the warriors would awake and go forth with the King to destroy all the enemies of the Cymry and establish Arthur's rule again in Britain. The stranger points to piles of treasure in the cavern and tells the drover that he can have as much as he can carry, but from one pile only. Also that should he ever accidentally sound the bell one of the sleepers will rouse, and say 'Is it Day?' Whereupon the answer must be given 'It is not day, sleep thou on.' The drover immediately begins cramming gold into his pockets and satchel, and looks up to find that the stranger has gone. He never sees him again.

The drover visits the cave many times to help himself to treasure. On occasion he accidentally rings the bell, but the awoken sleeper is reassured by the words and no harm befalls. Finally the drover neglects to say the correct formula, whereupon he is badly beaten by the guards and thrown out of the cave, never to find its entrance again.

The three versions of the theme share some ingredients, but each is a distinctive story. Many of the Welsh folk tales are like this. The legend of the Five Sleepers of Dolacauthi (or Dolaucothy, just off the A482, midway between Llandovery and Lampeter) tells of five saints who sleep in the galleries of the hillside gold-mines excavated in Roman times. They were the quintuplet sons of a servant of King Arthur, and sheltered in the mine during a storm. Laying their heads on stone pillows they went to sleep. They will not awake, it is said, until King Arthur reappears or 'a genuine and faithful apostolic bishop' occupies the throne at St David's. The unfortunate Gwen of Dolacauthi, led by the Devil, once paid a visit to the Five Sleepers, but was not made welcome. They imprisoned her forever in the cave, except at times of unnatural storm when her vaporous form is allowed out, and she is heard sobbing and crying far and wide. When the storm passes she has to return to the remote cave.

West of Llandeilo, on the way to Carmarthen, is the village of Nantgaredig. In the early years of the railway an elderly man named James saw a train in the small hours of the morning. Knowing that no trains were scheduled for this time he asked the station master about it the next day. The station master was puzzled, saying that for certain there had been no trains along the night before. A few days later a special train drew through the station bearing a large funeral party to Llandeilo. Mr James was convinced that he had seen a phantom funeral travelling by rail. Another portent from the same district was described in Howells's *Cambrian Superstitions* of 1831:

It is said that some years ago when the coach that runs from Llandeilo to Carmarthen was passing by Golden Grove (the property of the noble Earl

Cawdor) three corpse candles were observed on the surface of the water, gliding down the stream which runs near the road; all the passengers beheld them, and it is related that a few days after, some men were crossing the river near there in a coracle, but one of them expressed his fear at venturing, as the river was flooded, and remained behind; the other three, possessing less discernment, ventured, and when about the middle of the river, lamentable to relate, their frail conveyance sank through the weight that was in it, and they were drowned.

It was not only the countryfolk who were superstitious: on a certain market-day in 1824 the streets of Carmarthen were almost empty because a prophecy made by Merlin forecast a disastrous flood for that day. Most townspeople fled to Swansea.

On the western outskirts of Llanelli is Old Stradey House, haunted by the ghost of Lady Mansel whose unseen hands may play the organ music which seems to emanate from one of the thick walls.

A Grey Lady is said to appear on the slopes of Mynydd-y-Garreg, above Kidwelly, searching for her head. She was Gwenllian, the beautiful wife of Gruffyd-ap-Rhys-ap-Tudor, a twelfth-century Prince of South Wales who heroically led the Welsh against the Normans until she was captured with her young sons by the villainous Maurice de Londras who beheaded them all at a place called Maes Gwenllian.

On the other side of the Towy estuary a ghost once committed murder:

> The mother of Tomas ap Llywelyn ap Ywain, lord of Iskeod, was Annas, daughter of Tomas ap Robinod, constable of Llanstephan Castle. This Robinod came, with 21 Knights on white steeds to invade Korrws. . . . On the way he was met by the ghost of Gruffudd ap Rhys ap Phylip Vychan, who was nicknamed Gruffud Corr y Gyngrair, and his ghost killed Robinod on the road. (From 15th–16th-century Peniarth MSS.)

Laugharne is a small town full both of character and beauty (and there are only a handful of towns in Wales where that description would ring absolutely true). It is a place of pilgrimage for those who love the poetry of Dylan Thomas, and one can imagine the reaction of that boozy figure to the often bizarre pilgrims who flock to the place in summer. A few swear that they have seen his unmistakable ghost either at his home, the Boat House (his workroom was a shed with a view of the castle and river) or about the town. If so it is remarkable for there are also reports of him haunting a rehearsal room at the

Shepherd's Bush Hotel, London. Edward Thomas, possibly a greater poet, also lived at Laugharne; like Dylan he died in tragic circumstances being killed in one of the final actions of the First World War.

The most authentic ghost at Laugharne would seem to be that of a black dog which haunted the wayside pit at Pant-y-Madog. A young girl named Rebecca Adams who lived near the castle was sent to town one evening on an errand by her mother. Half-jokingly she warned her of the ghost of Pant-y-Madog. The girl was relieved to pass this point safely, but then out of the darkness loomed an enormous black dog, which gave a blood-curdling growl. Later, neighbours searching for the girl found her unconscious in the lane, and the black dog often returned to frighten other people who had to make the same journey. It appears to have been a harmless ghost, though, for nothing untoward ever happened to people who saw it. In olden days people believed that the fairies travelled to Laugharne from beautiful islands not far offshore. They would purchase goods at the market, always proferring the exact amount of money necessary for the goods, without being asked. Then they would return home by a secret subterranean tunnel.

At Green Bridge Cave, Pendine, the sound of ghostly violin music is occasionally heard. This is because an old fiddler, thinking that the acoustics inside the cave would flatter his playing, went inside. Unfortunately after his candle blew out he was never able to find the entrance and was lost forever. The smooth sands of Pendine were much-used after the First World War for attempts on the land speed record. It is surprising that the sounds of these cars do not linger, especially since the famous Welsh driver Parry Thomas was killed here, and his car buried in the dunes.

Haverfordwest is the capital of the Landsker, better known as 'Little England beyond Wales'. It was a distant outpost for the Normans too, who built the castle, but they inter-married more easily here and laid the foundation for the Englishness of the area that was to follow. Although the relationship between the Welsh and the incomers was generally better here, at times there were incidents which reflect the savagery of the times.

On one occasion the Governor of the castle captured a Welsh brigand and, having tortured and blinded him, held him in an informal sort of captivity. The Governor's young son used to delight in the tales that the prisoner told, full of adventure and romance, but a

LUCY BARLOW alias WATERS.

'The ghost of Roch Castle is the shade of Lucy Waters [Walters], first Mistress of Charles II' (*National Library of Wales*)

Haverfordwest.

deep hatred of his captors was in the prisoner's heart, and one day he grabbed the boy and holding him as a shield made his way to the battlements. The boy's father begged that the young life should be spared, but in vain, for the Welshman at length threw the child to his death and then jumped to destruction himself. Perhaps it is this man's ghost who was laid to dwell for a thousand years below Haverfordwest bridge 'in durance vile'. Since nobody knows when the thousand years began it is possible that the ghost will again come to trouble the town though no one knows when.

Five miles to the east of the town is Castle Gwys, better known as Wiston Castle. There is a legend that in the old days a serpent lived close to the castle which had a great many eyes, so that no one could approach it without being seen. At this time the succession of the estate was in dispute, and eventually it was agreed that anyone who could gaze on the dragon 'without the same serpent or cockatrice seeing him' should inherit the property. At length all the claimants but one had attempted to creep up on the wary serpent: none had been successful. But the last had thought up a plan of utmost cunning. He climbed into a barrel at the top of the hill above the dragon's lair, then came rolling down past the astonished beast saying 'Ha, ha! Bold cockatrice, I can see you, but you cannot see me!' This ingenuity

St Govan's cliffside hermitage (*National Library of Wales*)

enabled him to make a successful claim on the succession. Jacqueline Simpson remarks in her book *British Dragons* that 'it is pleasing, for once in a way, to read of a tale in which the hero need only outwit the creature, not slaughter it, in order to get his reward'.

On the other, western, side of Haverfordwest is Roch Castle, a small stronghold perched on a rocky crag which seems almost alien to the surrounding geology. Although in the last eighty years its owners have painstakingly restored the castle to its former glory, in the time of Marie Trevelyan it was a ruin. She tells the story of its first owner:

It is said that the feudal Lord of Roch built this solitary tower in a very peculiar place because he had been warned by a witch that his death would be caused by the sting of a serpent or adder. If he passed a certain year in safety he need not afterwards fear. When the tower was built the timorous Lord of Roch lived in the top storey of the stronghold. The year passed, and he was within a few days of his emancipation from thraldom. His friends prepared for rejoicings outside while he quietly but thankfully waited his release. It was cold and wintry weather, and the wind from St Bride's Bay set the prisoner's teeth chattering. The nights were so bitterly cold that a kind friend sent up a few faggots of wood so that the Lord of Roch might make a fire therewith, which he did 'right gladly'. The fire was quickly kindled, and the solitary man warmed his numbed hands. By-and-by he fell asleep, and from the embers on the hearth a treacherous adder crept up and stung the Lord of Roch. When his friends came the next morning he was dead.

The ghost of Roch Castle is the shade of Lucy Walters, first mistress of Charles II, who was born here in 1630. She floats through locked rooms in a white dress and may be the cause of the noisy running footsteps which mysteriously disturb the sleep of guests on occasions.

The coastline of the western extremity of South Wales is feared for its hazards by mariners (though it also offers a wonderful refuge in time of storm with Milford Haven). Throughout history the sea has been an important element in man's existence here. It was always possible to blend farming with the risky joys of fishing, smuggling, wrecking or even piracy, but the sea could take as well as provide, and there were many who met their deaths on the cruel and jagged rocks of Pembrokeshire.

Milford Haven (*National Library of Wales*)

We have met before with the 'cunning men' who would sell fair weather to sailors. The cunning man of Pentregethin in Pembrokeshire was different in that he sold foul winds if he could, favourable to the wreckers who rewarded him well if he was successful. This account of him appears in *The Folk-Lore and Folk Stories of Wales* by Marie Trevelyan:

> In Pembrokeshire there was a person commonly known as the cunning man of Pentregethen, who sold winds to the sailors, after the manner of the Lapland witches, and who was reckoned in the neighbourhood where he dwelt, much more than the divines; he could ascertain the state of absent friends, and performed all the wonderful actions ascribed to conjurors....

David Lewis of Eithin-duon in the parish of Trelech Cannar, sold both fair and foul winds, could raise storms and pass through keyholes at will. Trelech is some distance from the coast, so he must have worked powerful spells for sailors or wreckers to make the long journey to consult with him.

Even pirates could occasionally make disastrous mistakes. Some once stole the silver bell from St Govan's cliff-side hermitage. They were shipwrecked almost immediately, and sea-nymphs restored the bell to the holy man's cell, leaving it hidden below a rock on the edge of a well. When struck, this particular rock is supposed to sound with the sweetness of the silver bell. Close by is Huntsman's Leap, where the hunter, having made a successful jump across the chasm, returned to view his spectacular achievement and promptly died of fright! In the church of St Petrox there is a memorial to a lady who is supposed to return to the village as a headless ghost, riding in a carriage driven by a headless coachman and drawn by a headless horse.

A letter to the *Pembroke County Guardian*, 16 February 1901, tells of a succession of strange events that occurred aboard a naval vessel based in Milford Haven. The letter was written by Captain Alldridge who had taken over the paddle-steamer, the *Asp*, as a survey vessel in 1850. Before he undertook her command the *Asp* had been a civilian vessel, a packet carrying passengers between Donaghadee in County Down and Port Patrick in Scotland. He had accepted the newly refitted ship from a shipyard on the River Dee, and as he was about to sail the Dockyard Superintendent begged him not to take her out as she was haunted. All sorts of strange, unexplained noises had been heard as the shipwrights worked on the vessel: knockings, the sound of people rushing from one side of a cabin to the other, the noise of a drunken brawl . . . in addition one member of the gang had seen an apparition. Captain Alldridge disregarded all of this and made an uneventful voyage south to Martyn Roads, off Pembroke, where the ship was to be based. On the evening of her arrival there the look-out man saw the ghost of a lady standing on the paddle-box, pointing skywards.

Soon afterwards the ship was sailed upstream to Lawrenny, and on this short trip the captain's steward was actually spoken to by the ghost. He asked to be transferred to another boat. Few of the crew were able to endure the *Asp* for long, though the captain forced himself to put up with it for many years despite horrific experiences, including the ghost putting a clammy hand on his forehead as he rested in his cabin.

In 1857 the *Asp* returned to Pembroke Dock for repairs. One evening the sentry saw a dim shape moving towards him. As he challenged it he realised that it was the ghost. It walked through his musket. He shouted to alarm his three colleagues, and all of them were able to watch the ghost walk to the old churchyard within the dockyard where she vanished, never to be seen again.

The captain made enquiries about the history of the *Asp* before she was bought by the Navy. He discovered that after one trip between Ireland and Scotland a stewardess had found a beautiful girl in a berth in the ladies' cabin with her throat cut. Her killer was never found, and shortly afterwards the owners had offered the ship to the Navy.

The Realm of Faerie

The Welsh . . . a race for whom the insubstantial world has always been more real than the visible one, for whom the little people have always shaken their milk-white arms in a ring by moonlight and the towers of Avalon have always glimmered in the sunset. . . .
Bernard de Voto, American historian.

Fairy legends occur throughout Wales and the grandparents of many people living in the Principality today believed in their existence. Robin Gwyndaf collected this story from a farmer who spent his childhood at Ceunant, below Mynydd Cefn Du:

My brother and I used to go up to the top of a narrow little field where Taid (Grandfather) told us we had to hide and not show ourselves. There was a dry stone bank there about six feet high over which we could not see because we were too small. We used to take out stones very quietly from the wall and gaze through the hole. Within a few yards of us was the old Carreg Lefain which was like a piece of rock, and in the centre was a stone – when we were older we realized that this stone was an 'echo stone'.

It was in order to see the Fairies that we stood staring through the hole in the wall. The wind had turned and was coming from the east by now. It came through the hole in the wall till water filled our eyes. It was beginning to grow dark. After waiting a long time we saw the Fairies dancing round the stone – little things dressed in the daintiest many-coloured clothes you ever saw. Then we ran to Taid to tell him the story.

I was about eight-and-a-half years old when I saw the Fairies and my brother, Harri, was about ten years old. They were not more than two feet tall. They had many-coloured clothes like flowers and wore long caps with peaks high up on their heads. They looked like a garden of flowers on the move. They danced round the stone. We saw them simultaneously. We were frightened to disturb them, so we were as quiet as mice. Taid had warned us that if we showed ourselves it would not be well with us, and we would vanish. Perhaps we would sin against the Fairies too because we were watching them, you see. We were about fifty yards from the stone; we had made certain that we would be near enough to see and be able to hide from the Fairies at the same time. It was a pleasant time, about the end of August when the days were beginning to draw in. Taid used to tell us that it was in the evening that the Fairies appeared, when the sun was setting and when we were in the brooding silence.

'Fairies . . . who attended regularly the markets of Milford Haven and Laugharne. . . .'
(*Welsh Folk Museum*)

We had been there several times and had seen nothing. And that was the time we *did* see them. I cannot say whether we created this picture in our minds or not. That could have been very easy. But we *both* saw them. We dare not go there at night, and seeing them had made us frightened.

Taid used to say: 'Didn't I tell you that they were there? There you are, you are all right now!'

As I grow older I think a lot about these pleasant things.

Although people in Wales generally called them, *y tylwyth têg*, the beautiful family or tribe, this was a tactful expression that sometimes masked people's real opinion of them (dire trouble would follow if you were heard to be rude about the little people). Often they were mischievous or even malevolent, luring folk into woods or on to mountains to leave them lost, or even ill-treating them by making them dance in fairy rings until they were exhausted. It is probably a slanderous thought, but the excuse of being led astray by fairies might disguise a wealth of sins that would have brought the wrath of father, wife or husband down on the guilty.

Entrances to the fairy world were to be found near their dancing circles, in caves or ruined castles, or beneath boulders. Only on May Day could (or can, I have no reason to think that there are not fairies about nowadays) humans safely visit the fairy kingdom. If they are led there at any other time they will remain for a period of one, five, seven, or even a hundred years.

Some believed that they were 'the souls of virtuous Druids, who not having been Christians, could not enter into Heaven but were too good to be cast into Hell'. The varieties had their own names in Welsh:

> *Ellyll* was an elf.
> *Plant Annwn* were 'the children of the lower region'.
> *Gwrayedd Annwn* were fairy ladies or dames.
> *Gwlliaid* were goblins (particularly nasty).
> *Coblynau* were Knockers ('. . . a kind of good-natured impalpable people, not to be seen, but heard.' They are usually to be heard working in new mines and '. . . lead the men to the ore by knocking in its direction, and when the lode is reached the knocking ceases.'
> *Pwka* (Puck) were also invisible, and although good workers were also mischievous.

There were also regional variations, such as the 'Verry Volk' of Gower, which has a distinctly Devon ring to it. In Pembrokeshire they were the Fair Small People (*Dynon Bach Tég*), and it was believed there that they came from islands not far offshore.

> In some parts of Pembrokeshire and Carmarthen we have some singular accounts of *Islands* inhabited by fairies who attended regularly the markets at Milford Haven and Laugharne, bought in silence their meat and other necessaries and leaving money (generally *silver pennies*) departed, as if knowing what they would have been charged. They sometimes were visible and at other times invisible. The islands, which appeared to be beautifully and tastefully arranged, were seen at a distance from land, and supposed to be numerously peopled by an unknown race of beings. It was also imagined that they had a subterraneous passage from these islands to the towns. (Howells, *Cambrian Superstitions*)

Southey wrote that if you stood on a piece of turf cut from St David's churchyard and looked out to sea you would be able to see the enchanted islands where the fairies lived. There was another belief that in the country of the fairies there was a small piece of ground where a magical herb grew. This enabled the land to remain invisible even to the most keen-sighted invader, unless he happened to stand on this tiny patch with its remarkable plants. People spoke of the land of the fairies as being between Cemmes, the northern hundred of Pembrokeshire (to the south and west of Cardigan), and Aberdaron on the Lleyn peninsula.

Giraldus Cambriensis in his *Itinerary through Wales* which he undertook in 1188 wrote of the appearance and habits of the Tylwyth Têg:

These men were of the smallest stature, but very well proportioned in their make: they were all of a fair complexion, with luxuriant hair falling over their shoulders like that of women. They had horses and greyhounds adapted to their size. They neither ate flesh nor fish, but lived on a milk diet, made up into messe with saffron. They never took an oath, for they detested nothing so much as lies. As often as they returned from our upper hemisphere they reprobated our ambition, infidelities, and inconstances; they had no form of public worship, being strict lovers and reverers, as it seemed, of truth.

St David's Cathedral

It was not uncommon for mortal men to fall in love with, and even marry, fairy women. Although small (hopefully they stood taller than the twenty-four inches mentioned earlier) they made good wives as they were very beautiful 'and extremely active'. The drawback to being wedded to a fairy is that she was liable to be snatched back to fairyland at any time, if one was thoughtless enough to forget her origins. This story, *The Ystrad Legend*, comes from *Welsh Folk-lore: A Collection of the Folk-tales and Legends of North Wales* by Rev. Elias Owen, 1887. This book was the prize essay of that year's National Eisteddfod and won for the Rev. Owen a silver medal and twenty pounds.

In a meadow belonging to Ystrad, bounded by the river that falls from Cwellyn Lake, they say the Fairies used to assemble and dance on fair moon-lit nights. One evening, a young man who was the heir and occupier of this farm, hid himself in a thicket close to the spot where they used to gambol; presently they appeared and when in their merry mood, out he bounced from his covert and seized one of their females, the rest of the company dispersed themselves and disappeared in an instant. Disregarding her struggles and screams he hauled her to his home, where he treated her so very kindly that she became content to live with him as his maid servant,

Valley of the Mawddach (*National Library of Wales*)

but he could not prevail upon her to tell him her name. Some time after, happening again to see the Fairies upon the same spot, he heard one of them saying: 'The last time we met here, our sister *Penelope* was snatched away from us by one of the mortals.'

Rejoiced at knowing the name of his *Incognita*, he returned home; and as she was very beautiful, and extremely active, he proposed to marry her, which she would not for a long time consent to; at last, however, she complied, but on this condition – 'That if ever he would strike her with iron she would leave him, and never return to him again.'

They lived happily for many years together, and he had by her a son, and a daughter; and by her industry and prudent management as a housewife he became one of the richest men in the country. He farmed, besides his own freehold, all the lands on the north side of Nant-y-Bettws to the top of Snowdon, and all Cwmbrwynos in Llanberis; an extent of about 5000 acres or upwards.

Unfortunately, one day Penelope followed her husband into the field to catch a horse; and he, being in a rage with the animal as he ran away from him, threw at him the bridle that was in his hand, which unluckily fell on Penelope. She disappeared in an instant, and he never saw her afterwards, but heard her voice in the window of his room one night after, requesting him to take care of the children.

These children and their descendants, they say, were called *Pellings* – a word corrupted from their mother's name, Penelope.

The late Thomas Rowlands, Esq., of Caerau in Anglesey, the father of the late Lady Bulkeley, was a descendant of this lady, if it be true that the name *Pellings* came from her: and there are still living several opulent and respectable people who are known to have sprung from the *Pellings*. The best blood in my own veins is this Fairy's.

Thus far, most of the fairies that we have encountered have been either benevolent or relatively harmless. In contrast the Gwyllion were 'female fairies of frightful characteristics', who were more like witches in appearance, evil-faced, hunched-up hags well reflecting the derivation of their Welsh name, a gloomy goblin. Their delight is to lead astray those in peril on mountains: anyone lost in mist or darkness on a lonely mountain path seeing the hazy outline of an old woman in a grey dress would be certain to become lost even though they knew the path well before seeing the figure. Travellers would struggle to catch up with the Old Woman of the Mountain but no matter how much they hurried she would remain ahead, finally vanishing with a cackle of unholy laughter.

The story of the recent film *Labyrinth* is that of evil fairies stealing a child: this theme could have been taken straight from Welsh tradition except that when fairies steal a human child in Wales they invariably leave one of their own kind in its place – the Changeling. Welsh fairies seem to favour stealing blond children, so every precaution should be taken to safeguard fair-skinned babies particularly. They should be baptised as soon as possible and protected by wearing crosses made of iron or rowan.

Stories of Changelings come from all over the world – after all it was a convenient way to explain sub-normal or deformed children, especially in societies where there was much interbreeding or even incest. In Wales the Changeling is the *plentyn-newid*, and at first the mother fails to notice that it is not her own baby that she is nursing, so exact is the replica that has been left. But within days the child changes: it grows ugly and shrivelled and there is 'something diabolic in its aspect'. A hundred years ago it was said that the Changeling usually lived longer than such children normally do, reaching the age of ten or twelve, but to do so it might have had to survive a number of cruel tests akin to those that suspected witches were put to. It might be placed on a shovel and held over the fire, bathed in a tincture of foxglove (which gives us the stimulant digitalis: a baby was killed by foxglove poisoning in Caernarvonshire in 1857) or it might be starved to death. All these cruel tests were meant to find out whether or not the child was mortal, or to persuade the fairies to restore the human baby. On one occasion in Glamorgan they apparently worked. The Virgin Mary appeared to the mother and told her to prepare a meal for

all the household and servants in an egg-shell: this would make the baby speak. She did this and the Changeling asked her what she was up to. Being told he exclaimed:

'A meal for ten, dear mother, in one egg-shell? I have seen the acorn before I have seen the oak: I have seen the egg before I saw the white hen: I have never seen the like of this.'

To this the mother replied that for certain he had seen too many things, and that he should have a beating, whereupon 'the child fell to bawling, and the fairy came and took him away, leaving the stolen child sleeping sweetly in the cradle.'

This story is from Wirt Sykes's *British Goblins*; Sykes was the American Consul in Cardiff in the 1870s, and from the same source comes this final story of the perils of being enchanted by fairies.

Shon ap Shenkin was a young man who lived hard by Pant Shon Shenkin *(in Carmarthenshire)*. As he was going afield early one fine summer's morning he heard a little bird singing, in a most enchanting strain, on a tree close by his path. Allured by the melody he sat down under the tree until the music ceased, when he arose and looked about him. What was his surprise at observing that the tree, which was green and full of life when he sat down, was now withered and barkless! Filled with astonishment he returned to the farmhouse which he had left, as he supposed, a few minutes before; but it was changed, grown older, and covered with ivy. In the doorway stood an old man whom he had never before seen; he at once asked the old man what he wanted there.

'What do I want here?' ejaculated the old man, reddening angrily; 'that's a pretty question! Who are you to insult me in my own house?'

'In your own house? How is this? Where's my father and mother, whom I left here a few minutes since, whilst I have been listening to the charming music under yon tree, which, when I rose, was withered and leafless?'

'Under the tree! – music! what's your name?'

'Shon ap Shenkin'.

'Alas, poor Shon, and is this indeed you!' cried the old man. 'I often heard my grandfather, your father, speak of you, and long did he bewail your absence. Fruitless inquiries were made for you; but old Catti Maddock of Brechfa said you were under the power of the fairies and would not be released until the last sap of that sycamore tree would be dried up. Embrace me, my dear uncle, for you are my uncle – embrace your nephew.'

With this the old man extended his arms, but before the two men could embrace, poor Shon ap Shenkin crumbled into dust on the doorstep.

Dyfed, West and North

The legend of the fairy kingdom situated off the Pembrokeshire coast seemed to take on a new significance in 1977 when witnesses swore that they had seen vehicles looking like spacecraft drive up to the Stack Rocks in St Bride's Bay. Great doors opened in the rock and the craft vanished inside; small figures were seen on the rocks soon afterwards.

This report was just one of an incredible series that began in March of that year and continued into the summer. It generated nationwide, even worldwide, publicity and several books were written on the sightings, amongst them *The Dyfed Enigma* by Randall Jones Pugh with F. W. Holiday and *The Welsh Triangle* by Peter Paget. At first sight it may seem that UFOs fall outside the scope of this book, but since the mystery of their origin has never been solved and some of the reports had supernatural nuances, it would be unworthy to ignore a modern phenomena which has the makings of a legend.

The Close Encounters began on 4 February 1977 when children in the playground of Broad Haven School were able to watch a spacecraft which had landed in a field opposite. It was the lunch-break, and unfortunately the headmaster ignored the pleas of the children to come and look at the silvery-yellow, cigar-shaped object which was fascinating them. Their vehement assertions to parents attracted press interest, however, and within the week the report was being investigated by UFO experts. Just thirteen days later there was a second incident, this time witnessed by adults. They saw a similar cigar-shaped object which glided off with a humming noise, but more importantly the teacher and two canteen workers also saw a figure climb out of the vehicle. Again the location was close to the school, and careful investigation proved that the UFO could not have been mistaken for any sort of a wheeled vehicle as the ground was too boggy: however there was no evidence to show that anything had been there.

On the evening of 13 March a young man was returning home on foot when he saw a glowing, oval object in the sky at Hendre Bridge. Just afterwards he was startled by a large black dog which padded past him silently and seemed to come from the direction in which he had seen the UFO. His way home took him past RAF Brawdy by the perimeter fence, a lane he knew very well. As he passed a gateway which led into the airfield he realised that he could not see the lights of the RAF station: some enormous object was blocking the view. He strained his eyes to look closer and saw a great dome-shaped object, at least twenty feet high, with a faint glow round its edge. He thought it must have been between thirty and forty feet wide. As he gazed in bewilderment he saw a strange figure approaching. It was tall, dressed in an almost-transparent suit, and had a strange head (not a helmet) with very large eyes set like those of a fish. Since it moved aggressively towards him he took a swing at it, failed to connect, and, terrified, ran most of the way home. When he got there the dog, usually the most friendly of animals, barked and would have nothing to do with his master.

Tall faceless figures were also seen with, presumably, a spacecraft at the Haven Fort Hotel at Little Haven. The hotel is built on the site of a fort which protected St Bride's Bay against invasion and is haunted by a White Lady. When it was suggested to the lady who saw this humanoid shape that it was someone from the RAF station dressed in an anti-radiation or chemical warfare suit she wrote indignantly to the newspaper:

> I write to comment on the photograph on the front page of the *Western Telegraph* (12 May) headed 'The Thing'. Your picture bears not the slightest resemblance to the two faceless humanoids I recently saw in my field alongside a UFO which was pulsating a very bright glow and lighting the surrounding area. I can assure all your readers and any sceptics that on the evening in question I was neither drunk nor am I the type of person to imagine things. *I saw exactly what I reported.*

The lady had been disturbed in the first place by her radio suddenly going off whereupon she heard a strange humming noise. Getting up to look out of the window she saw what she described above. After this incident questions were asked by a local Member of Parliament and it was disclosed that an atomic shelter stood close to where the space ship had been seen.

There were numerous other sightings during that year, some more convincing than others. Although the rational explanation may be that the Ministry of Defence were up to weird and wonderful tricks, it remains an intriguing mystery to many of those who investigated the matter closely. The authors of *The Dyfed Enigma* conclude:

> Strange spaceman-like figures appeared to people all over Pembrokeshire in

that spring of 1977. They were seen by children as young as eight and by pensioners. These figures had an apparitional quality in that they did things which are impossible in terms of physics . . . they would float in mid-air or disappear while under observation. They and their craft or vehicles seemed to be massless and therefore unaffected by gravity. . . .

If it is true that UFO events recur every ten years, 1987 should also be a significant year (see also page 142).

One other incident from this district which is macabre but might have supernatural repercussions: in 1791 the *Increase* of Scarborough ran ashore at Druidston Haven. Naturally all the villagers hurried down to the beach to gather in this unexpected harvest of the sea. Unfortunately the *Increase* had been carrying a cargo of gunpowder, and when something of metal was thrown from the wreck on to the beach it hit a boulder and lit a spark which caused a terrible explosion and fire. It was the women in their long skirts who suffered worse, and beside eight people being killed many of the villagers bore powder scars for the rest of their days.

Tufton is a remote village at the foot of the Preseli Mountains. It must have been an even lonelier place during the last war at the time of this story which was told to Robin Gwyndaf:

I myself saw an apparition once, in the light of day, when I was about twelve years old. I was in Cwmslade, a small-holding in the district of Tufton, with Ron Stevens, training hawks, during the summer holidays. At that time there was an American army camp in Cas-mael with over a thousand men. From Cwmslade I could see over the mountain and the tanks were shooting targets. All was dust and red flames, you see, blue flames too. We were feeding hawks behind this little cottage, the tiniest little cottage I have ever seen, with windows no more than the size of matchboxes. I used to spend the evenings with Mr Stevens who was an Englishman. I didn't have much English in those days, but he understood me and I understood him. The Welsh I taught him was more than the English he taught me, and that's the truth for you.

Well! I was feeding these hawks now, you see, behind that little cottage. I had a hawk on my hand − here − and I had a rabbit's leg. Stevens was at the far end of the garden, over there. And we had hawks out on those little perches. The back of the garden was all hedge, all of it a thorn hedge. The thorns began to move, and the hawks now began to be alarmed. Good gracious me! a black dog emerges from those thorns. But they were too thick for anything to come out of them. They were too thick for a rabbit, and Mr Stevens said:

'Frighten the dog away, Dick.'

I went up to it and cried 'Wssh!'

When I said it a big black woman rose up right in front of my eyes with a black hat on her head. Her top teeth curled out right over her bottom lip. All her clothes were black but she had white teeth. Her hands were encased, as though in gloves, and were tight across her chest. There were big black boots, with their toes curling up, on her feet. When I was half turning back again I looked at her and there was a big old smile on her face. We followed her for about twenty yards and more, Ron Stevens and I, for Stevens was like me, moving forward, mesmerised. We could not talk at all, only stare at each other. She was half turning round and drawing us on, and we followed. She went out through a little gap, a little hole, in the garden. On the left, outside the garden, was a well in the ground, you see. We peeped into the well. The water had not stirred. We had lost her in the well. Inside the well was an empty bottle. It kept milk cool because it was summer and it saved the milk from going sour, you see. Nothing at all had moved. Well now, we had had a fright, oh boy, yes. You won't believe what a dreadful fright we had had.

Right away I went with the hawk, yes, and home. I went straight for home, through all the bog in the field. I usually went round it. And when I arrived home mother was washing the floor in the passage. I fell and collapsed in front of mother on the floor. After that I was in bed for a fortnight after the fright. That's the biggest fright I ever had.

Mr Gwyndaf adds some footnotes to the story. No one subsequently lived at Cwmslade; the Forestry Commission took over the land and later demolished the cottage. It had been one of the loneliest cottages in the district, which was why it was so suitable for training hawks. The well had not been more than two feet deep, but that is where she disappeared. Mr Stevens had moved out of the cottage that evening and had never returned. There was no talk in the village about anything untoward having happened there and Mr Harries, the storyteller, did not know of anyone else who had seen a ghost there. He had not told his story to anyone for fear of ridicule. For all that this is a haunting without a cause, it remains a compelling story with the ring of truth to it.

Newcastle Emlyn is a small market town about ten miles east of

'Corrupt and greedy, Sir Herbert Lloyd of Peterwell'
(*National Library of Wales*)

Cardigan. It has two castles, both well ruined. Cilgerran is majestically situated above the River Teifi where salmon fishers still use coracles on occasion. The younger castle is in the town itself; slighted by Cromwell, it is a romantic ivy-covered ruin. A wyvern, the two-legged variety of dragon, used to dwell in this latter castle. Its anti-social habits (it was a fire-breather) led a certain brave soldier to shoot it. In order to distract its attention he threw a piece of red flannel into the river, which the wyvern immediately attacked (it was well known that dragons, like bulls, were infuriated by anything red). This gave the soldier the opportunity to shoot the wyvern through its only vulnerable place, the navel, for they are elsewhere protected by a tough leather carapace. Jacqueline Simpson *(British Dragons)* suggests that it is unlikely that these beasts would have navels and that the storyteller demurely used navel as a misnomer for the wyvern's vent: 'If one has imagined a reptilian monster covered all over with impenetrable scales, then the vent and the open mouth are indeed the only two places available for a successful attack.' It might be thought that its eyes too were vulnerable.

The story of a powerful curse comes from Lampeter. In the seventeenth century the Vicar of Llandovery had a son who fell in love with a daughter of the Lloyds of Maesyfelin whose mansion was situated on the other side of the river from the town. One day her brothers returned unexpectedly and found the two lovers *in flagrante delicto*. Seizing the young man they tied him head downwards to his horse and sent it off galloping home on the hill road to Llandovery. The youth was dead by the time he reached Llandovery: his heartbroken father then prayed a curse on the family of Lloyd and the house of Maesyfelin.

Although they abandoned Maesyfelin the family appears to have flourished at first, and in the early eighteenth century Sir Herbert Lloyd had a splendid new house built near by, Peterwell, complete with a roof garden. Sir Herbert was the epitome of an evil landlord. Corrupt and greedy, he violently desired anything that was denied him. Above all, one trifle rankled him. By fair means and foul he had cleared tenants and freeholders from all the lands that surrounded his new house, with the exception of a smallholding that he could see from the fabulous roof garden. This belonged to Shon Philip who had farmed the land for generations. Shon Philip was a good old man who, helped by his wife, toiled hard to earn his living from the few fields. Nothing that the wicked Sir Herbert could offer would induce the old

'Cilgerran Castle is majestically situated above the River Teifi'
(*National Library of Wales*)

farmer to leave his birthright, and so in the winter of 1762 he thought of a ploy to rid him of Shon for good.

He began by spreading a rumour that one of his valuable black rams had either been stolen or had strayed from his flock. His men were sent about the district searching for it. Then one dark night two of them climbed up on to the roof of Shon Philips's farm with the ram and dropped it down the broad open chimney. Unhappily for them, the elderly couple were not disturbed from their slumbers.

When his men returned to Peterwell and reported that things had gone to plan, Sir Herbert sent one of them for the parish constable (by now it was three in the morning) and led the puzzled man to Shon Philip's house. Since Sir Herbert was the magistrate a warrant to search the house was at hand, and at last the farmer and his wife were awoken by the noisy party at the door. What they made of the sooty, half-crazed animal that was raging about the house is not recorded, but the squire's plan had worked and jubilant with success he had both of them locked away forthwith. The next day the treacherous Sir Herbert offered Shon Philips a pardon if he would sell his land, but the old man stubbornly refused once more and so the couple were taken to prison at Cardigan. The trial was a foregone conclusion. Although all the district knew of the way that the old people had been framed people feared the wrath of Sir Herbert so much that none would stand against him, and Shon Philip was executed outside the town. A few days later Sir Herbert produced a deed of conveyance to the land which he swore bore the assent of the innocent victim to the baronet's ownership.

There was no end to the villainy of this evil man, and at one time Sir Herbert was the most powerful man in the county. But at length his extravagance took its toll, and once decline set in his fall was hastened by the multitudes that he had wronged. Stung by a sermon preached against him he left Lampeter for London, and, his fortune dissipated and his body decayed by venereal disease, he shot himself at his favourite gambling den in London. However even in death his troubles were not over. His corpse was sent back to Wales and laid in the great hall of his house to await burial the next day. But bailiffs managed to gain entry and pinned a notice on the coffin forbidding internment until all debts had been paid. They guarded the coffin day and night, from August into September. By this time the stench must have been almost intolerable, and the impasse was only overcome by the wicked baronet's servant plying the guards with drugged ale. At dead of night the body was buried.

Thus, it was said, the old curse was at last redeemed, for the old stones from Maesyfelin had gone into the making of Peterwell.

Sir Herbert Lloyd had earlier had an interest in another property in the north of the county – Hafod, close to Devil's Bridge. Like Peterwell it had a chequered history which finally ended in the 1950s when the ruins of the last great house to be built on the site were pulled down and replaced with a caravan site. In Sir Herbert's time Hafod was owned by Thomas Johnes, a Shropshire landowner. Shortly after Lloyd's death (and possibly triggered by its circumstances) he began to build a palace in this lonely, but incredibly beautiful valley. The sad and romantic story of his dream home is told in *Peacocks in Paradise* by Elisabeth Inglis-Jones, a memorable book now hard to come by.

But it was the original manor-house at Hafod that was haunted. It was let to a tenant named Paynter who was almost as debauched a character as Lloyd himself. Paynter was the manager of Lord Powis's mines at Esgair y Mwyn, and must have had some fine feelings to recognise the great beauty of Hafod's mountain setting, surrounded by rich woodland. The house had been troubled by a poltergeist previously, in 1751, when the *Bwgan yr Hafod* became notorious:

> . . . at first the ghost did not meddle with fire or salt, but would carry stones, vessels and other articles about the house and hand various tools to persons according to their crafts. Potatoes in a basket ready for boiling jumped out one after the other to the ceiling, no more to be seen until they returned into the basket, 'as you have seen maggots jump out of cheese in hot weather'. A company of 15 being in a room shut close, the hearth was filled with stones. A person put his foot on one stone to keep it secure. All the stones, including the one under the man's foot, were removed to the other end of the room. A hall table, as much as four men could lift, would be turned feet upwards, knocked against the ceiling, and instantly replaced. When the mistress called for a tub with oatmeal, it was thrown on to the table without spilling a grain. A parson who attempted to control the ghost had his head broken till the blood ran, and a piece of painted delf ware came gently on to a person's plate. The master's greatcoat would be put about a chair and buttoned up, two or three pieces of peat placed on top for a neck and a hat a-

The last great house to be built at Hafod (*National Library of Wales*)

'The Devil . . . had a hand in the construction of the Devil's Bridge. . . .'

top of that. When the old man hit them down in a passion, the buttons would open and the coat be thrown after him. Sometimes a big coffer would be laid athwart the bed over his legs.

Welsh Folklore and Folk Custom, T. Gwynn Jones

After an eight-year lull, the disturbances resumed when the new tenant, Paynter, came to the house: the ghost became amorous. No doubt this reflected a little on Paynter's own lifestyle, for he was a famous lecher and the entire household was 'notably disreputable'. The ghost would fondle and kiss girls in the dark and at first there were many who believed that it was Paynter taking advantage of the ghost's reputation to pursue his own desires. But then it materialised into a beautiful woman and was about to kiss him when it abruptly turned into the shape of a pig, rubbing around his legs. This behaviour occurred in front of his wife (whom the Bwgan never troubled) and other witnesses until Paynter became so frightened of it that he finally called in a wizard from Brecon who laid the ghost for the payment of one hundred pounds. After that nothing more was heard of the Bwgan yr Hafod.

The Devil, as the name implies, had a hand in the construction of the Devil's Bridge which is not far from Hafod. He built it for an old woman in order to rescue her cow from danger. His condition was that he should have the first thing to cross the bridge. She threw a crust across and a small dog ran across the bridge to get it. Those intending to cross the bridge at night were urged to take with them a Crucifix or a Bible otherwise a terrifying apparition would come up behind them to push them off the bridge and into the tumult of the pools far below, from where they would be sucked to the gates of hell.

One unlikely story tells how the Bwgan that haunted Hafod originated as a goblin in the hotel at Devil's Bridge. Since the first hotel on this site only came into being at the time of the building of the mansion this is obviously nonsense, unless it was the Bwgan yr Hafod which came to the hotel.

A local wizard was called in to lay this troublesome goblin and first turned it into a bulldog, then a frog, and finally into a fly, which rested for a fatal moment on the wizard's book of spells. The book was quickly slammed shut and the ghost laid in the waterfall together with an ounce hammer and a tintack. Should the ghost ever succeed in cutting a fathom of rock with these tools it will be released.

Back to the seaside again, this charming description of an encounter

90

with a mermaid comes from J. Ceredig Davies's *Folk Lore of West and Mid-Wales*:

In the month of July, 1826, a farmer from the parish of Llanuwchaiarn, about three miles from Aberystwyth, whose house is within 300 feet of the seashore, descended the rock, when the sun was setting beautifully upon the sea, and he saw a woman (as he thought) washing herself in the sea within a stone's throw of him. At first he modestly turned back; but after a moment's reflection thought that a woman would not go so far out into the sea, as it was flooded at the time, and he was certain that the water was six feet deep in the spot where he saw her standing. After considering the matter, he threw himself down on his face and crept on to the edge of the precipice from which place he had a good view of her for more than half-an-hour. After scrutinizing her himself, he crept back to call his family to see this wonderful sight. After telling them what he had seen, he directed them from the door where to go and to creep near the rock as he had done. Some of them went when they were only half dressed, for it was early in the morning, and they had only just got up from bed. When the wife came on, she did not throw herself down as the others had done, but walked on within sight of the creature; but as soon as the mermaid saw her, she dived into the water, and swam away till she was about the same distance from them as she was when she was first seen. The whole family, husband, wife, children, menservants and maidservants, altogther twelve in number, ran along the shore for more than half-a-mile, and during most of that time, they saw her in the sea, and sometimes her head and shoulders were upwards out of the water. There was a large stone, more than a yard in height, in the sea, on which she stood when she was first seen. She was standing out of the water from her waist up, and the whole family declared that she was exactly the same as a young woman of about 18 years of age, both in shape and stature. Her hair was short, and of a dark colour; her face rather handsome, her neck and arms were like those of any ordinary woman, her breast blameless and her skin whiter than that of any person they had seen before. Her face was towards the shore. She bent herself down frequently, as if taking up water, and then holding her hand before her face for about half-a-minute. When she was thus bending herself, there was to be seen some black thing as if there was a tail turning up behind her. She often made some noise like sneezing, which caused the rock to echo. The farmer who had first seen her, and had had the opportunity of looking at her for some time, said that he had never seen but very few women so handsome in appearance as this mermaid.

Nanteos is a handsome Georgian mansion built between 1739 and 1757 by the Powell family. It is chiefly famous for the wooden cup claimed to be the original Holy Grail, used at the Last Supper. Originally lodged at Glastonbury Abbey, at the Dissolution it was taken secretly to Strata Florida Abbey, but when Henry VIII's soldiers approached that remote monastery it was hidden at the former house at Nanteos. The vessel is supposed to have supernatural powers of healing, though these may have become diminished over the centuries as splinters have been taken from the cup as relics. The house has three ghosts: an early Mrs Powell who is manifested as a Grey Lady holding a candelabra to warn when the head of the house is about to die; that of a lady who left her deathbed to hide jewellery which has never been found; and a phantom horseman who rides up the gravel drive late at night.

Finally, on the outskirts of Aberystwyth itself, there is a headless dog which haunted Pen Parcau about a hundred years ago. It may be connected with the legend of a young giant of the district who, seeing his father in distress, rode off at such a rate to rescue him that the dog's head came off in the leash.

Powys

Powys covers a vast area of Mid-Wales, from the Brecon Beacons in the south to the Berwyn Mountains in the north. Within this area there are no very large towns, but many of a comfortable, manageable, size, like Brecon, where it is just about possible to avoid people you don't wish to meet.

Mr Gwyn Evans recently met with a ghost in the living quarters above his Welsh Bookshop in The Struet. An asthma sufferer, he was accustomed to getting up in the small hours. On one such occasion, as he was making himself a drink, he was startled to see the dim figure of a woman in the apartment. She was dressed in eighteenth-century clothes and glided across the room to pass through the wall into the house next door. At first Mr Evans doubted his own senses, thinking that this might have been a waking dream, but soon afterwards, in similar circumstances, the same events recurred. He said nothing about his experiences but visited a previous owner of the shop and gently directed the conversation towards things ghostly. Without prompting he learnt that the ghost had often been seen, not only in his own house but in the one next door, where the disturbing sound of children crying was also heard. In the nineteenth century the bookshop had been the Surgeon's House so many harrowing experiences had been enacted there; otherwise there is no explanation for the haunting.

Another ghost I was told of in Brecon was also without explanation. A military gentleman was sharing a cottage on the outskirts of town with a girlfriend. Sleeping alone, one night he heard the latch of his bedroom door click and then felt an almighty thump on his shoulder. Sitting up he saw a woman at the end of his bed brushing her hair. He realised that she must have hit him with the hairbrush. Hurriedly he put on the light whereupon the woman vanished. He settled into an uneasy doze and then again heard the door open, dragging over the carpet. This time the apparition was of a woman in a wheelchair – the same woman, but now she was *old* and was not wearing a long dress. The owner of the cottage identified the description of the woman as her grandmother but could not think of a reason for her appearance.

An older Brecon story is set at the Roman camp on the north bank of the River Honddu, about three miles from the town. A man weary from travelling rested for a while here until he caught sight of a

'Brecon, where it is just about possible to avoid people you don't wish to meet'
(*National Library of Wales*)

beautiful grey horse which seemed to be begging to be ridden. However as soon as he mounted the animal the traveller realised that he was on the back of no ordinary horse, but a *Ceffyl y Dwr*, or water-horse, which, on a mad tour of South Wales paused only once at a place that the traveller could identify (it was near Carmarthen) before returning him to the Roman camp three days later 'in a worse state than when he had left, for the Ceffyl-dwr had dragged him through mire and water, through brambles and briars, until he was scarcely knowable'.

Llangorse Lake, the legend goes, was once the site of a large city which had a reputation for wickedness and debauchery. The local king sent an ambassador to the place to see whether the dreadful reports of the city were true. He arrived in the evening but there was no one to greet him, and the sounds of drunken revelry came from the centre. Entering into a cottage at the outskirts he found it deserted apart from a sleeping baby. Inadvertently he dropped a glove into the baby's cradle. He then left the city to spend the night on a hillside overlooking it. During the night he heard terrible sounds from below

– thunder, the clash of arms, shrieking and crying, and the dashing of waves. Morning light revealed that the lake now covered the site of the city, the only sign of life being a child's cradle bobbing on the waves. When it drifted ashore he found that it held the baby, and his glove.

The Last Witch of the Beacons, 'a princess of Druid blood' used to haunt Llyn Cwm Llwch – The Devil's Pool – on Carn Du which is one of the highest summits of the Brecon Beacons. The pool was said to be bottomless but is actually only about twenty feet deep. The story was retold in *Tales and Traditions of Breconshire* by Stanley Jackson Coleman:

There once roamed on the steep side of Carn-ddu a wild woman, a descendant of the Druids, possessing all their magical lore. She had no shelter wherein to rest, but wandered without ceasing night and day 'with eyes that hath not power to close' as the old Welsh poem says. A witch, she had the Devil as her father. Her age no one could tell. She had been handed down from father to son as an immortal which no one saw and lived to see again. As she roamed thus in her strange restless manner, she sang as ever did the sirens, and, like them, drew a crowd of admirers to their doom. One word alone from her could save them from destruction when once they saw

'No ordinary horse, but a *Ceffyl y Dwr*, or water-horse'

'Mol Walbee was said to have built the castle at Hay-on-Wye in a single night'
(*National Library of Wales*)

that look of unutterable age upon her face. That word she never uttered, save once. A traveller on these lonely heights was drawn to her: she lured him on slowly with her sweet music until at length he fell worn out on the banks of the Devil's Pool. Then, bending over him, repeating these mysterious words '*Naw cant o'ddynion marw, naw cant, naw cant*', she cast the remains of the poor maddened stranger into the pool. This was the fate of every stranger, lured, maddened, and cast into the pool, since the translation of the weird incantation is '*Nine hundred dead men, nine hundred, nine hundred!*' and her spell was an ancient one which averred that if she, or her like, placed nine hundred dead persons of either sex into the pool, she would have the powers of making a human being fall in love with her. Thus alone could she regain her youth and beauty – for she had once had them!

This hag, thus far, resembles the evil fairies, the *Gwyllion* (whose purpose was to lead travellers astray), as much as any witch. Her fate, however, betrays her evil origins.

One day the lovely Princess Eira fell victim to the hag's irresistible music. Her lover, Prince Bran-Credugion, swore to wring the secret words from the witch, and so set about attempting to encounter her. Sure enough, he met her on the mountain, but failed to escape the charm of the fatal music. But the witch, about to tip him into the pool, looked long at his face and realised that she was in love with him. But she was unable to remember the words that would release him from the paralysing spell. In desperation she summoned the Devil, and at this all those who she had thrown into the lake rose up, screaming and writhing, with the Devil himself. Amongst them was his Princess, but when offered her freedom she rejected the Prince (awakened now from the spell), clinging instead to the Devil. The Prince was utterly broken by this, and seizing the witch climbed to the precipice of Pen-y-Pen where he jumped to destruction, taking the last witch of the Beacons with him.

Mol Walbee, who was said to have built the castle at Hay-on-Wye in a single night, was also reputed to be a witch. She was, in fact, Maud de St Valerie, the wife of William de Breos, Lord of Brecknock and Abergavenny. Because of her courage, her enormous size and alleged occult powers she was thought to be able to achieve miracles, however this did not prevent a terrible fate for herself and her children. When she became too 'stomackful' in her opposition to the dealings of the wicked King John he had her and her son entombed alive at Corfe Castle with just a piece of raw bacon and a sheaf of wheat. After eleven days both were found dead.

Hay-on-Wye, with its countless fine bookshops, is one of the most interesting of small Welsh towns. Presteigne is hardly less appealing. It has an imposing parish church where thirteen parsons gathered in the seventeenth century to exorcise the evil spirit of Black Vaughan of Hergest Court which troubled the neighbourhood. When, holding lighted candles, they successfully summoned him to appear twelve of them were so frightened that they fainted. The thirteenth continued with the exorcism, eventually transforming the ghost of Black Vaughan into a bluebottle and trapping it in a snuffbox. It was then committed to eternal rest in Hergest Pool. A black dog that roams the hills around the town is said locally to have been the inspiration for Conan Doyle's *Hound of the Baskervilles*, though the author himself claimed that the idea came from a Dartmoor spectral hound. A blemish on the character of Presteigne was the execution, in 1805, of a girl of seventeen who had killed her new-born baby. Also up to the 1850s it was possible to buy a wife at market at these country towns of the Borders, the husband often leading his spouse into town at the end of the rope. In one instance the farmer, having sold his wife for a shilling, generously threw the rope in with the bargain.

The last dragon to be killed in Radnorshire died at Llandeilo Graban, south of Builth Wells. It had for a long time been the terror of the surrounding countryside until it was lured to its destruction by a ploughboy, who had been attracted by the large reward offered to the person killing the beast to try his luck.

He made a dummy-man out of a large log of oak and, aided by the local blacksmith, armed it with numerous iron hooks, powerful, keen and barbed. Then he dressed the dummy in red and fixed it firmly on top of the church tower. At dawn the following day the dragon first saw his daring bedfellow and dealt him a violent blow with his tail, which was badly torn by the hooks. Infuriated by the pain, he attacked the dummy with tooth, claw, wing and tail, and finally wound round his wooden foe and bled to death.
(*Radnorshire* by W. H. Howse)

A parallel story from Llanrhaedr-ym-Mochnant in the north of Powis tells how a standing stone known as the Post Coch (Red Pillar) got its name because the people of the village once draped it with red cloth and studded it with concealed spikes 'in order that a flying dragon should batter itself to death against it'.

Llanidloes is in Montgomeryshire, set in lonely, beautiful countryside between Aberystwyth and Newtown. The story of Lady Jeffrey's Spirit comes from the Rev. Elias Owen's *Welsh Folk-lore*, published in 1887.

This lady could not rest in her grave because of her misdeeds, and she troubled people dreadfully: at last she was persuaded or enticed to contract her dimensions, and enter into a bottle. She did so, after appearing in a good many hideous forms, but when she got into the bottle, it was corked down securely, and cast into the pool underneath the Short Bridge, Llanidloes, and there the lady was to remain until the ivy that grew up the buttresses should over grow the sides of the bridge and reach the parapet. The ivy was dangerously near the top of the bridge when the writer was a schoolboy, and often did he and his companions crop off its tendrils as they neared the prescribed limits for we were all terribly afraid to release the dreaded lady out of the bottle. In the year 1848 the old bridge was blown up, and a new one built instead of it. A schoolfellow, whom we called Ben, was playing by the aforesaid pool when the bridge was undergoing reconstruction, and he found by the river's side a small bottle, and in the bottle was a little black thing, that was never quiet, but it kept bobbing up and down continually, just as if it wanted to get out. Ben kept the bottle safely for a while, but ere long he was obliged to throw it into the river, for his relations and neighbours came to the conclusion that that was the very bottle that contained Lady Jeffrey's spirit, and they also surmised that the little black restless thing was nothing less than the lady itself. Ben consequently resigned the bottle and its contents to the pool again, there to undergo a prolonged, but unjust term of imprisonment.

From the same source comes another story of the laying of a restless spirit, that of Cynon, a wicked goblin who plagued the lonely Llanwddyn Valley long before it was filled with water for the benefit of the citizens of Liverpool. It is now known as Lake Vyrnwy. Cynon's restless and mischievous spirit was at last laid by the famous sorcerer Die (or Dick) Spot, who trapped it in a quill which was placed under a large stone in the river below Cynon Isaf. This stone was called 'Careg yr Yspryd', or the Ghost Stone. There it was to remain 'until the water should work its way between the stone and the dry land'. Work on the reservoir began in 1881 and it became necessary to divert the river away from the Ghost Stone, which had to be removed. Confronted with this huge boulder, which weighed close on twenty tons, the workmen decided to use explosives to demolish the obstacle whereupon all the local workers chose to leave the scene as they feared the fury of Cynon's spirit. The first charge left a smallish boulder about four feet in height. A second charge was set to this, and when the smoke cleared the surface of the small pool of water in which the stone had stood was seen to boil violently, and out of it hopped a frog, rubbing its eyes. All of the workmen avoided the place for as long as they could afterwards, and at night sounds of heavy chains being dragged across the uneven ground came from where the rock had been.

The story of the Powis Castle Ghost was famous in the nineteenth century – 'one of the most singular tales of the appearance of a ghost'. The events took place sometime before 1760, at the Earl of Powis's great castle at Welshpool. 'A poor unmarried woman, who was a member of the Methodist Society, and become serious under their ministry' had visited the castle to see if she could work there for a while spinning home-grown hemp and flax for the household. She had done this before at Powis and was generally offered accommodation while she was working. 'The quality' were away in London, and she was surprised to be shown to a grandly furnished bedroom on the ground floor where a fire burned brightly and a candle stood on the table. As the servants left the room she was surprised to hear the lock click on the door, and disappointed to think that they lacked trust in her. She settled down to read her Bible before bedtime, but was disturbed by hearing the door open. Before her stood a gentleman in a gold-laced hat and waistcoat who walked across the room to a window and stopped there, looking out for some time. Then he returned across the room to the door, opened it, and walked out, closing it behind him. Again she heard the click of the lock. Although she knew the family by sight she could not recognise the features of this gentleman. Puzzled and more than a little frightened, she knelt down to say her prayers. As she knelt the gentleman returned, walked to the window and then left the room as before, again without speaking. By now she was convinced that she had been in the presence of a ghost and that the servants had given her this room on purpose knowing it to be haunted. She decided to speak to the ghost if it appeared again. When, after a short time, it did so, she said: 'Pray, sir, who are you, and what do you want?'

The ghost told her to take her candle and follow him; he took her to a small room, and when she hesitated at the threshold he assured her that no harm would come to her but that she should observe his

Powis Castle presented 'one of the most singular tales of the appearance of a ghost' (*National Library of Wales*)

The grave on which the grass will never grow (*Welsh Folk Museum*)

actions. Then he stooped and lifted one of the floorboards. Beneath was a box with an iron handle, and stepping across the room he pointed out a crevice where the key was concealed which would open the box. He spoke earnestly to her: 'This box and this key must be taken out and sent to the Earl in London. Do this and I will trouble the house no more.'

The poor woman promised this eagerly, the ghost nodded and walked out of the door, never to be seen again. Immediately she roused the servants, explained what had happened, and the box and key were sent off to London. When the Earl received these, and learned of the way in which they had been found, he rewarded the poor spinning woman well, setting her up comfortably on his estate at his own expense. Only Lord Powis ever knew of the contents of the box, but the ghost never reappeared so it must have been satisfied at the outcome of its mission.

Montgomery is a former county town where time seems to have stood still; apart from bungalows around the outskirts, few new buildings have been put up since 1821 when the body of John Newton Davies was buried in the churchyard. There is some dispute as to what crime it was that led Davies to the gallows, some say murder, others theft, but there is general agreement that he was innocent, whatever it was. At the time of his execution, while he still protested his innocence, the sky darkened unnaturally and the most unholy storm was let loose on the town. John Newton Davies's grave is still in the churchyard, and although many attempts have been made to remedy its state, grass has never been grown on it successfully. The Rector told me that it is believed that misfortune has always followed those who have attempted to cultivate the grave. One straggly rosebush grows there now, but before this the bare earth clearly made the pattern of the Cross.

South Gwynedd and Lleyn

The Happy Valley is the name of the valley of the little River Dyffryn which a minor road follows for much of the way from Towyn to the Dovey Valley at Pennal (it could be named the Aberdovey by-pass). Behind the hillside to the south of this road (look for the National Park car park) lies tiny Llyn Barfog, in bygone days a place well liked by fairy tribes. There were famous green elves here, lady fairies who kept a herd of milk-white cattle called Gwartheg y Llyn, or cattle of the lake. These fairies were undoubtedly members of the tribe called *Gwagged Annwn* (or *Gwragedd Annwn* in Sikes's *British Goblins*), ancestors of the Tylwyth Teg, and the most beautiful of the Welsh elves. This is the description of them given in *A Field Guide to the Little People* by Nancy Arrowsmith and George Moorse:

> Tall, proud, blonde and immortal, they live in rich palaces under Wales' many lakes, coming to land to dance, hunt or just stroll around, two or three at a time. On full-moon nights they rise from the ground a minute before midnight and dance lightly in the meadows until the first cockcrow in the morning. On many of these nights, only their heads can be seen, bobbing up and down over a soft field of silver mist.
>
> The Gwagged Annwn are a very old race and for some reason not explained in legend are predominantly female. Because of this, they often look to handsome young men for companionship. The marriages between humans and Gwagged usually end unhappily for men, for the lake maidens only marry on difficult terms. For example, their husbands must never touch them with iron or hit them in any way, however lightly. Many young men marry them anyway, for their beauty is irresistible. Children of these unions are gifted with magic powers, and the elf women's dowries of fat lake cattle are rich prizes for penniless farmers.

However their alleged inability to count beyond five must have made it difficult for them to allocate this dowry. But let us return to the fairy cattle of Llyn Barfog.

One day an old farmer of the district managed to catch one of these fat cows, 'which had fallen in love with the cattle of his herd'. From that day the farmer prospered, he had fat calves, butter, cheese and milk of a richness not before dreamed of, and became the wealthiest man of those mountains. But one day he was fool enough to decide that his fairy cow was getting old and should be fattened up and slaughtered.

Llyn Barfog

The cow was tethered, regardless of her mournful lowing and her pleading eyes; the butcher raised his bludgeon and struck fair and hard between the eyes — when lo! a shriek resounded through the air, awakening the echoes of the hills, as the butcher's bludgeon went through the goblin head of the elfin cow, and knocked over nine adjoining men, while the butcher himself went frantically whirling around trying to catch hold of something permanent. Then the astonished assemblage beheld a green lady standing on a crag high up over the lake, and crying with a loud voice:

> *Come yellow Anvil, stray horns,*
> *Speckled one of the lake,*
> *And of the hornless Dodin,*
> *Arise, come home.*

Whereupon not only did the elfin cow arise and go home, but all her progeny to the third and fourth generations went home with her, disappearing in the air over the hill tops and returning nevermore. Only one cow remained of all the farmer's herds, and she had turned from milky white to raven black. Whereupon the farmer in despair drowned himself in the lake of the green ladies, and the black cow became the progenitor of the existing race of Welsh black cattle.

The upper reaches of the Dovey Valley are truly a land apart, and as the surveyor Christopher Saxton observed in the early seventeenth century, 'it so riseth with mountaines standing one by another in plumps, that as Giraldus saith, it is the roughest and most unpleasant country to see to, in all Wales'. Today we regard this area as one of the most lovely parts of North Wales, but the scenery is strikingly different from that of Snowdonia or other mountainous areas. Here the hills are steeply sided, of even height, criss-crossed by a maze of streams which have etched deep valleys. Saxton also noted that the inhabitants of the district had a bad name amongst their neighbours, 'for being too forward in the wanton love of women'. Their typical physical characteristics – the men were tall and strongly built, with coppery hair rarely to be found elsewhere in Wales – and their lawlessness gave them the reputation of being Brigands, or red-haired banditti, as Borrow called them. The reputation was not ill-founded, for they were for long the scourge of the district until in 1554 Sir John Wynne of Gwydir rounded up their leaders and eighty of them were sentenced to death by Baron Owen. One of the mothers of the condemned men cursed the Judge as he passed sentence – the old woman bared her breasts and shrieked: 'These yellow breasts have given suck to those who will wash their hands in your blood' – and sure enough his party were ambushed on Christmas Day near Mallwyd as they returned from the Assize at Montgomery. There were thirty arrows in the Judge's terribly mutilated body, and the spot where the ambush occurred (on the A458 where it runs through a ravine by the Dugoed stream, close to the hairpin bend, about two and a half miles from Mallwyd) may still be heard to echo with the cries of his death agony.

Cader Idris, or the chair of the giant Idris, is reputed to be the haunt of good fairies, but the dark lake that lies at the foot of its southern escarpments, Llyn y Cau, is said to be the haunt of a monster similar to that of Loch Ness. It once snatched the body of a swimmer brave or foolhardy enough to attempt to swim across the lake.

Moel Offrwm, a lesser height to the east of Dolgellau, is the 'hill of offering or sacrifice', where legend has it that human sacrifice was offered by Druids in the dark ages of Wales. The victims were thrown from the top of the great cliff that overlooks the mansion of Nannau, once the historic home of the Vaughan family.

The story of the *Ceubren-yr-Ellyl*, the 'hollow tree of the Spirit' is the most famous legend of Nannau. Hywel Sele was Lord of Nannau in the time of Owain Glyndŵr; he was also Glyndŵr's cousin, but opposed him in that he supported Henry VI. In 1402 Glyndŵr visited Nannau to try to win Sele's support for his rebellion, and together they walked in the Deer Park. The Lord of Nannau was never seen again alive, but about forty years later his skeleton was discovered in the hollow trunk of a great oak that had been struck by lightning. This oak tree survived until 1813, when on a hot, sultry night it toppled to the ground, and the ghost of Hywel Sele, which had haunted Nannau over four centuries, was never heard of again.

The ghost of a lady seduced by one of the ancient Lords of Nannau haunts the crossroads where the drive from the mansion crosses the Dolgellau to Llanfachreth road to reach the Deer Park. He killed her, with her pet dog, when she became demanding. It is said that many years ago the head kennelman awoke in the middle of the night to hear his dogs baying and howling. When he left his cottage to investigate he saw the figure of a lady in a long dress accompanied by a little dog as he approached the crossroads. He followed them until both disappeared by a small stone bridge. When the place of their disappearance was thoroughly investigated the skeleton of a woman was found, with that of a dog. Quite close to this spot is a place called Ffynnon-y-mulod, the Mules' Well, where a groom once took a stallion from Nannau to water. Daffodils surrounding the watering-place were suddenly disturbed by a gust of wind causing the stallion to shy violently, dragging the groom down and then trampling him to death. At night time when the daffodils are in bloom the sounds of this accident are heard again – the shouts and groans of the dying man and the snorting and whinnying of the stallion.

There are several legends attached to Llyn Cynwch, the lovely lake above Nannau. It is said that there was once a dragon that caused so much havoc in the district that the Lord of Nannau offered a reward of sixty cattle to anyone who could kill it. A shepherd named Meredith discovered the beast asleep by the lake, and, leaving his two dogs to guard it, hurried to Cymmer Abbey to borrow an axe. Courageously he fought the dragon with the axe, his dogs helping him, and eventually overcame it. This is remembered in a name for the hill above the lake – Carnedd-Bedd-y-Wiber or The Grave of the Serpent.

'The "hollow tree of the spirit" is the most famous legend of Nannau.'

Another legend of this lake tells how a young man on his way to visit his sweetheart took a short cut by way of the shores of Llyn Cynwch. In the darkness he fell from the path, into the icy waters of the lake. As he sank down he suddenly realised that he was able to breathe without difficulty, and arriving at the bottom found himself in a land of great beauty. A little man greeted him and took him to a magnificent palace where he was put at ease by Lords and Ladies in resplendent clothes and treated to a lavish banquet. At last he remembered his sweetheart and said farewell to his new friends, and the little man who had earlier guided him took him to a long flight of steps. Climbing these he came to a trapdoor which opened into the very hearth of his lover's house. She was delighted by his unexpected appearance, for although he thought he had only been away for a few hours, in fact it was many months since he had disappeared.

A more sinister aspect to Llyn Cynwch is the man-shaped monster which drags itself from the water crying 'The hour is come but not the man', and if anyone happens to be near he will be dragged below the surface of the lake and never seen again.

Llyn Tegid at Bala also has a monster which lies curled up at the bottom waiting for the unwary. Legend has it that the old town of Bala was swamped when the keeper of the spring that supplied it with water forgot to put its cover on. It is also said that the new town will suffer the same fate.

On the hillside which overlook the eastern, upper shores of Llyn Cwm Bychan are the famous Roman steps across which the Romans are said to have led their pack animals. The ghosts of miners of Roman times, and Roman soldiers, are supposed to have been seen here (east of Harlech).

About nine miles to the south of Harlech is the lonely hamlet of Egryn, in 1905 the scene of 'the most remarkable series of phenomena ever reported in Wales'. The Egryn lights seemed to follow a revivalist preacher, Mary Jones, who was the wife of a farmer who lived at Egryn. She had become a convert of Evan Roberts, a young evangelist who claimed to see visions of angels. Like Roberts, Mary Jones said she received messages from Christ himself; but uniquely others were able to share her experiences by witnessing signs of the visitations themselves. Although they were unable to see the personification of Jesus that Mary Jones experienced, very many people were able to see the strange lights that her presence seemed to generate. The first press account appeared in the *Cambrian News* of 13 January 1905:

> Last week Mrs Jones attended a meeting at Pensarn, where hundreds of people congregated. The chapel can be seen from the railway and as a train, driven by a Machynlleth man, was passing, a strange light was seen shooting out of ten different directions, and then coming together with a loud clap.
>
> 'Never do I wish to see anything like it again', said the driver in relating his experience. Both he and his mate saw the light.

Mary Jones's notoriety soon spread, and the lights seemed to become brighter and more numerous. It was noticed that lights rested on the roofs of certain houses, and where they did so the inhabitants were certain to become converts shortly afterwards. Soon Mary Jones was attracting great numbers of people to her daily meetings in the chapel at Egryn; she also attracted the interest of the national newspapers. This account came from the *Daily Mirror*'s correspondent who had travelled back from a meeting in company with Mrs Jones:

> For three miles we had driven in silence, and I had given up hope. It was close on midnight and we were nearing Barmouth when suddenly, without

the faintest warning, a soft shimmering radiance flooded the road at our feet. Immediately it spread around us, and every stick and stone within twenty yards was visible, as if under the influence of the softest limelight. It seemed as though some large body between earth and sky had suddenly opened and emitted a flood of light from within itself. It was a little suggestive of the bursting of a firework bomb – and yet wonderfully different. Quickly as I looked up, the light was even then fading away from the sky overhead. I seemed to see an oval mass of grey, half-open, disclosing within a kernel of white light. As I looked it closed, and everything was once again in darkness.

Many explanations have been offered for these phenomena. Did Mary Jones induce the visions by auto-suggestion? Could marsh-gas have caused them? (her chapel was situated on the marshy coastal plain by the railway), or were the lights carried by hoaxers? A modern theory suggests that they were UFOs. The *Barmouth Advertiser* unearthed an obscure reference from the early nineteenth century which told of similar events having occurred before:

'The Moors above Bettws-y-Coed'

'Tis creditably reported that in the year 1692 a fiery exhalation was seen to cross the sea, and set fire to the ricks of hay, corn and barns near Harlech, and to infect the grass, but was not mischievous to men, though they were in the midst of it. It proceeded in the night from the same place for some months, commonly on Saturdays or Sundays. The only remedy to extinguish or drive it away was to sound horns or trumpets, or to discharge guns.

The fervour of the revivalists also created more predictable phenomena. Many of the converts saw visions as well as lights, and more than a few were to end up as permanent residents of mental institutions. As a local newspaper put it

> *If these things you see and hear,*
> *Sometimes distant, sometimes near*
> *Don't you seek to reconcile 'em,*
> *They'll do that in the Asylum!*

The lights seem to have faded away as the days grew longer in the early months of 1905. Mary Jones's fame lessened accordingly, and the passionate days of the revival were over by the end of the year. Although she continued as a Sunday School teacher at the little Egryn Chapel Mary Jones sponsored no more remarkable occurrences, and she died in obscurity in 1936. The events of 1905 remain one of the mysteries of Wales.

Two miles to the south-east of Talsarnau is Maes y Neuadd, a two-star Country House Hotel which incorporates part of a fourteenth-century house where Cromwell is supposed to have stayed. Robert Graves described this as the most haunted house he had ever known: its ghosts are usually seen in mirrors, the exception to this being the little yellow dog which walks on the lawn early in the morning.

The following story comes from the Rev. Elias Owen's *Welsh Folk-lore*; shameful to relate, I cannot exactly locate the lake in question, though believe that it is either on or near the Lleyn peninsula.

There is a lake in Caernarvonshire called *Llyn-Nâd-y- Forwyn*, or the Lake of the Maiden's Cry. It is said that a young man was about to marry a young girl, and on the evening before the wedding they were rambling along the water's side together, but the man was false, and loved another better than the woman whom he was about to wed. They were alone in an unfrequented country, and the deceiver pushed the girl into the lake to get rid of her to marry his sweetheart. She lost her life. But ever afterwards her

Spirit troubled the neighbourhood, but chiefly the scene of her murder. Sometimes she appeared as a ball of fire, rolling along the river Colwyn, at other times she appeared as a lady dressed in silk, taking a solitary walk along the banks of the river. At other times groans and shrieks were heard coming out of the river — just such screams as would be uttered by a person who was being murdered. Sometimes a young maiden was seen emerging out of the waters, half naked, with dishevelled hair, that covered her shoulders, and the country resounded with her heart-rending crying as she appeared in the lake. The frequent crying of the Spirit gave to the lake its name, Llyn-Nâd-y-Forwyn.

The same author also tells of an old woman who lived in a tumble-down little hut on the foothills of Snowdon in south Caernarvonshire. She was generally avoided since she was believed to be a witch, but her grandson, who lived with her, was famous with the gentry as, if there was to be coursing done, he was certain to find the hare. But the hare that he started was never caught though the pursuit was always long and exciting, and the lad was always rewarded with his shilling. Eventually the sportsmen became suspicious and consulted a conjuror or wizard, who explained that it was his opinion that the hare was, in fact, a witch, who would only be caught by a black greyhound. The countryside was searched for such an animal, and at last one was found and brought to the next coursing. The hare was released and the black greyhound gave chase.

'Hei! ci du', shouted the sportsmen at their black dog, urging it on.

'Hei! Mam gu', shouted the lad, forgetting himself by cheering on his grandmother.

The greyhound was within inches of the hare throughout the chase. Finally, with an enormous leap, the hare jumped through the window of the old woman's hovel, but not before the greyhound has taken a bite at the flying animal — it had a piece of skin in its teeth when it returned to its master. The huntsmen immediately opened the door of the cottage and there was the old women sitting peacefully by the fire, but beneath her chair was a pool of blood. As Giraldus Cambrensis remarked in 1185:

It has also been a frequent complaint, from old times as well as in the present, that certain hags in Wales, as well as in Ireland and Scotland, changed themselves into the shape of hares, that, searching teats under this counterfeit, they might stealthily rob other people's milk.

Maentwrog Bridge (*National Library of Wales*)

The Lleyn peninsula is most akin to Gower or west Pembrokeshire. Its position makes it a great danger to shipping, for in the days of sail it was easy to get trapped before a south-westerly, which would inevitably blow a ship on to these shores unless the captain was a genius. The great strand at the tip of Lleyn is called Hell's Mouth, reflecting the age-old threat it held for sailors. Just inland from this beach is Gelliwig, where the Llanengan parson had a terrible struggle in exorcising an evil spirit. The spirit objected to its terms of imprisonment in a hole drilled in the beam of the house. The parson intended that it should stay there for fifty years, the spirit held out for ten. In the end the British love of compromise prevailed and the ghost was confined for twenty years. Afterwards the parson's clothes were in tatters and he stank so greatly that he had to be washed from head to toe with soft soap.

At Aberdaron, at the tip of Lleyn, overlooking the holy isle of Bardsey with its 20,000 saints, there was a famous healing well in the cave of Ogo Vair. It was believed that anyone who managed to take a mouthful of its water up the 'circuitous and dangerous path' to the top of the cliff would have any wish they cared to make fulfilled.

Another circuitous and dangerous path led down to the quarry village of Nant Gwrtheyrn, on the north coast of Lleyn. This remains a wild place, even in these days of motor transport. Centuries ago, the legend tells, three holy men came to the original tiny village here to attempt to convert it to Christianity. However the head of the village was a pagan, and drove them away at first with stones and then with abuse. At the top of the long climb back up the cliffs the three priests paused and each in turn lay a curse on the place. No one born in the village should be buried in consecrated ground, said one: neither male or female born there should ever marry with another born in the village, said the second: while the third holy man decreed that the village of Nant Gwrtheyrn would at last die, and become ruinous and deserted.

From that time misfortune and disaster dogged Nant Gwrtheyrn. The menfolk of the village fell prey to all sorts of accidents, being mainly drowned as they fell from boats or cliffs. Most of the women, frightened by the curse, left the place to live elsewhere: young women invariably picked husbands from a different community. Thus there were few people who had the need for burial, and those that did had to lie in unconsecrated ground. Then two of the young people of the village fell in love, and in defiance of the curse they decided to marry. They followed all the ancient traditions of marriage, exchanging presents on the morning of the wedding, the bride giving a puppy to the groom. Then she left her house to hide, for it was the custom that the bride should pretend shyness and have to be caught by the groom and his supporters. Expecting a token pursuit, the hunt began light-heartedly, but after some time had elapsed it became desperate. By nightfall the bride still had not been found, but the groom continued seeking her, for day after day, even after the rest of the village had accepted that she had fallen into the sea and drowned. He paced the shore for months, holding the dog that she had given him, demented, alone. The villagers at last found that the dog he held in his arms had died long since as he had neglected to feed it, and when this last consolation was taken away from him the young man threw himself into the sea.

Many years later there was a great storm which brought one of the oaks on the cliffs above Nant Gwrtheyrn crashing down. The force of its fall split open its trunk, which disgorged a skeleton wearing fragments of a bridal gown.

There was little trace of the original village of Nant Gwetheyrn when quarrying brought a new purpose to the place. The new villagers built neat houses, a school and a chapel. But the prosperity lasted less than a hundred years and then the place fell into decay again, becoming in the early 1970s one of the last resorts of the Flower People, which led to the 'Ghost Village' featuring in the scandal sheets. Yet now the village is reviving again: tourists trudge down the steep incline to visit the rebuilt houses which are now occupied by artists and craftsmen. Do the residents today remember the curse? What will happen if a lady weaver falls in love with a gentleman potter? No doubt we will read about it in a Sunday tabloid if such a thing does come to pass.

North Gwynedd and Anglesey

The Aberglaslyn Pass is the main route into Snowdonia from the south. It is an impressive entry into a mountainous region. A steep ravine, hung with fir trees, looks upon the tumbling waters of the Glaslyn, on their way to meet the sea at Porthmadog. In high summer crowds trample the banks of the stream until the grass can only struggle to stay alive. On the far side of the river walkers make their way along the old railway line, through the two tunnels that either delight or horrify young children. In these conditions it is hardly a place where a ghost might be expected to flourish, but in the small hours of a winter's night, making your way through the narrow defile on foot, it would still be easy to think that either the White Lady of Aberglaslyn, or the huge mastiff which used to frighten travellers here, could lurk around the next bend. The White Lady is a particularly inauspicious ghost to meet with: she only appears to those who will suffer an unexpected accident or sudden death.

Beddgelert is certainly the most beautiful mountain village of Wales, if not in all of Britain. Its name is probably derived from the sixth-century Saint Celert – 'the burial-place of St Celert' – but the alternative fable has appealed to so many dog-lovers over the last two centuries that it is impossible to resist the temptation to retell it:

Llywelyn *(the Great)* during his contests with the English had encamped with a few followers in the valley, and one day departed with his men on an expedition, leaving his infant son in a cradle in his tent, under the care of his hound Gelert, after giving the child its fill of goat's milk. Whilst he was absent a wolf from the neighbouring mountains, in quest of prey, found its way into the tent, and was about to devour the child, when the watchful dog interfered, and after a desperate conflict, in which the tent was torn down, succeeded in destroying the monster. Llywelyn returning at evening found the tent on the ground, and the dog, covered with blood, sitting beside it. Imagining that the blood with which Gelert was besmeared was that of his own son devoured by the animal to whose care he had confided him, Llywelyn in a paroxysm of natural indignation forthwith transfixed the faithful creature with his spear. Scarcely, however, had he done so when his ears were startled by the cry of a child from beneath the fallen tent, and hastily removing the canvas he found the child in its cradle, quite uninjured, and the body of an enormous wolf frightfully torn and mangled lying near. His breast was now filled with conflicting emotions, joy for the

'The Aberglaslyn Pass . . . is an impressive entry into a mountainous region'

preservation of his son and grief for the fate of his dog, to whom he forthwith hastened. The poor animal was not quite dead, but presently expired, in the act of licking his master's hand. Llywelyn mourned over him as over a brother, buried him with funeral honours in the valley, and erected a tomb over him as over a hero. From that time the valley was called Beth Gelert.

(*Wild Wales* by George Borrow)

The legend appears to have been invented by David Pritchard, the owner of the Goat Hotel in the latter years of the eighteenth century, to boost the tourist industry. It was certainly a remarkably successful ploy which has endured far longer than millions of others subsequently inflicted on us in the name of public relations. As well as having a flair for these matters Mr Pritchard also had a supernatural talent. He is supposed to have haunted Room 29, returning a hundred years after his death to tell the staff of money hidden beneath the hearthstone.

Pritchard's deception was revealed in 1899 by D. E. Jenkins in *Bedd Gelert, Its Facts, Fairies, and Folk-lore* which also warns of the Brown Hobgoblin:

This was one of the day-goblins, and generally appeared to lonely wayfarers when crossing from one district to another over mountain tracks. He would appear in the form of a rustic, clad in homespun and corduroy, wearing nothing on his head, and carrying a long stick like that of a shepherd. He invariably walked in front of the traveller, with his back towards him, but not on the ordinary path. He would keep alongside of the path, and would thus gradually draw his follower out of the way. After he had drawn the wayfarer far enough from the path, he would suddenly disappear behind some wall or heap, leaving his dupe in great perplexity and utter ignorance of his whereabouts.

This goblin would sometimes descend from the montains into the glens and valleys, and would strut along the walls in the fields, and along the roadside; he would now and again pop his head over the hedges to look into the roads. Thus parents frequently warned their children not to loiter on their errands for fear that 'Bwbach Llwyd' would see them.

More fearsome than this hobgoblin was Brenin Llwyd, the Grey King or Monarch of the Mist. He was supposed to sit amongst the mountains clothed in grey clouds and mist, waiting to eat up anyone

Snowdon, haunt of Brenin Llywd, the Grey King (*National Library of Wales*)

who became lost on the peaks. When climbing mountains first became popular with the gentry the guides who were paid to accompany them were genuinely terrified of Brenin Llywd and would never venture away from the recognised paths, much to the frustration of their clientele.

One of the most sinister spots on Snowdon is Glaslyn, the lake below the summit of Snowdon. Its name comes from its green colour caused by the presence of copper lodes. An afanc, or water monster, is supposed to lurk in its murky depths. It came from Llyn yr Afanc on the River Conway, where it had so troubled the neighbourhood that drastic steps were taken to stop its depradations. It was tempted from the pool by a beautiful girl and then captured by villagers. Instead of killing it they decided to commit it to the most remote place they knew, and so harnessed teams of oxen and dragged it across country to Glaslyn. Close by is another tarn containing a troublesome spirit: the account is again from *Bedd Gelert, its Facts, Fairies and Folk-lore*:

One skilled man thus related his perilous experience in laying a ghost on one occasion when he had mistaken the grade of the troubler. 'You have heard speak of the ghost of Erw,' said he; 'it was an awful ghost, one of the worst that I have ever heard of. He became so exceedingly troublesome that the family had to give up the house, which was closed for some years in the hope that the ghosts would go away. But on seeing that this did not avail, and that instead of becoming better the ghost became much worse, the man came to me to ask my advice. I promised to go and put him down.

'One evening – I shall never forget it – I went thither, and entered the house; I then made the mystical circle on the floor with salt, and drew the image of the cross in its centre. Then I entered the circle myself and stood between the arms of the cross in the customary way, reading the usual charm passage. Almost instantly the door is flung back, and some hideous creature, not unlike a huge tiger, enters, gnashing its terrible teeth at me. It then turned around the circle, as much as to say, "I have got thee now." I immediately perceived that I had mistaken its grade, and that I had used too low a summons. But I stood like steel before him, showing not the slightest bit of fear, and ordered him to withdraw in the name of the cross on which I stood, or else that I would curse him with endless torture. He stood unmoved, and there we remained for a long time staring at one another, until at last I could see him gradually withdrawing. I then instantly changed one word in the charm passage, and he came back, licking the floor like a dog before his master. I pronounced his sentence and sacrificed him to the bottom of Llyn Du; and while there is water in that lake he will never come forth to trouble any one again. That was the last spirit with which I had to do, or will have to do. If I had betrayed the least bit of fear, or if I had taken my eye off for the quarter of a second, I would have been done for.'

The final story from the Beddgelert district comes from the collection of folk tales collected orally by Robin Gwyndaf and translated by him. It tells of the Witch of Hafod Lwyfog.

My father had relatives living on a farm called Hafod Lwyfog, in Nant Gwynant, still there today on the left as you go from Beddgelert up to Hafodydd Brithian. And on that farm there were two daughters, very pretty girls. Their skin was like alabaster. Everybody talked about their beauty.

They slept in the same room. One morning one of them said to the other, 'Good gracious me! What's the matter with your face?'

'Why?' said the other.

'My! you have scratched yourself, or something, last night.'

'Oh no!' said the other, looking in the mirror and she sees the scratches on her face.

'Don't you say anything', said her sister, 'because your face is exactly the same. You have scratches too.'

And they laughed thinking no more than that some insect had come into their bedroom, since they lived on a farm.

Well, a few weeks went by, and good gracious me, the same thing happens again. But this time there was more blood on their faces. Their father and mother now started to wonder what was the matter, and they said to the maidservants and manservants:

'Well! are you sure that the cats and dogs were out last night and that no one came into the house?'

'Yes', was the answer.

'Well then, you must make quite sure from now on that there is nothing in the house, because there is something doing this, as this is the second time and as there are more scratches on their faces.'

What they did was take special care the last thing at night that there were no cats in the house. They had three or four on the farm to catch mice, and one of the servants would stay up all night to keep watch. When they saw nothing happening they all went to bed and slept.

Just about the same space of time passes and for the third time the same thing happened. Only this time the scratches were deeper and there was more blood on their faces again. The father and mother did not know what to do now. There was no policeman in the district nearer than Porthmadog or Caernarfon, and anyway they didn't feel there was much point telling a policeman. They were very worried indeed because they didn't know whom to ask for help. They knew very well that it was not one of the family nor any of the servants who made the scratches on the girls' faces. In the end they went and told an old man what was happening.

'Listen', said he, just like that. 'There is a conjurer living in Denbigh. He could give you some help about what to do.'

And they went to see this wise-man. They told him what had happened from beginning to end, the three times, and he said to them:

'It's a person who does it. I can't tell you whether it's a man or a woman, but it *is* a person. And this is how you'll find out who it is. There's something wrong with one eye, but I don't know which. Do you understand? That's how you'll recognise the person'.

Then whenever any stranger came to the farm they would say: 'That's the person', and stare and laugh. One morning however a shepherd came to the village, but not to the farm. He had been up Snowdon doing something to the sheep for it was lambing time. That was also the time when there were eagles on the mountains. If a lamb died eagles would go for its eyes immediately. The shepherd told the people of the village:

'Dear me!' like that, 'something strange happened this morning. I saw a woman's body on Snowdon, and what was odd was that her two eyes were wide open. She hadn't been dead long or the birds, the eagles, would have taken her eyes. And she was only skin and bones.'

Of course men went up to bring the body down. They had no idea who the woman was, but an aged man in the village remembered something and he said: 'She is an old maidservant of Hafod Lwyfog.' And when he thought back he remembered that someone had said there was a maidservant once in Hafod Lwyfog who had gone out at night and had never come back. They searched for her in the two lakes, Gwynant and Dinas, and everywhere else to find out where she had gone. They did not know who her family were and they never found her. She had gone as though the ground had swallowed her, as people said: and that's it.

However, there was no doubt now in their minds that this body was the maidservant's, and that she had died on Snowdon. She had fallen in love with the son of Hafod Lwyfog and maybe he did not want to have anything to do with her. And that is why she went away and disappeared. She must have been jealous, terribly jealous of the two girls. What she had done was go to the house and she knew every hole and corner having been a maidservant there. The old man was old enough to remember, too, that there was something wrong with one of her eyes, and that's how they found

The Fairy Glen, Bettws-y-Coed

out who the dead woman was – for, because her two eyes were open they could see that there was something wrong with one of them.

After she had run away the maidservant had lived in a cave on Snowdon. She had come from that district and knew everywhere on Snowdon. She would come out at night and would milk the cows and take swedes and carrots and other vegetables from the fields. That explained why she was so thin and old-looking. She never came out in the daytime. Because she had been a maidservant in Hafod Lwyfog she knew where to find the sisters. She wanted revenge and she got it by disfiguring the girls' faces so that they would never again be beautiful. But the girls recovered because the scratches had not been deep enough.

Nothing happened after the body was found. The girls were left in peace, and the maidservant came to be known as 'the Witch of Hafod Lwyfog'.

Betws-y-Coed is the main tourist centre for the east of Snowdonia, with plentiful souvenir and craft shops, hotels and eating houses. It is a pleasant enough place, set on the Afon Llugwy amidst richly forested hills, but the traffic on the A5 is noisy and relentless as it passes through the village. The Swallow Falls are about two miles from Betws-y-Coed, also on the A5. It cannot be an easy resting-place for the spirit of Sir John Wynne, though his lifetime is said to have been as turbulent as the place where his spirit is bound. His bad reputation may have come about partly because of his achievements, as Yorke points out in his *Royal Tribes of Wales*: 'Being shrewd and successful in his dealings, people were led to believe he oppressed them. It is the superstition of Llanwrst to this day that the Spirit of the old gentleman lives under the great waterfall, Rhaiadr y Wennol, there to be punished, purged, spouted upon, and purified for the foul deeds done in his days of nature.'

The next story takes us further eastwards on the A5 to an inn that was situated between Betws-y-Coed and Cerrigydrudion. It was a place notorious for its robbers. Guests would retire to their rooms, sleep soundly after a hard day on the road, and awake in the mornings to find the door still securely bolted but their valuables gone. Having lost a considerable sum of money in this way one traveller consulted with Huw Lloyd of Cynvael, Festiniog, a man who was famous for his wisdom (he was also vicar of Cynvael and lived between 1533 and 1620).

Huw had been an officer in the army, and, dusting off his old uniform and sword, decided to act the part of an army officer

124

travelling to Ireland. The inn was kept by two sisters intimidating both in their appearance and manner, but Huw succeeded in charming them by recounting his many adventures abroad. At last he stretched, yawned, and begged to be allowed his bed. It was always his custom, he said, to have candles burning overnight, and this was agreed. He settled down to watch the night away.

Ere long two cats stealthily came down the partition between his room and the next to it. Huw feigned sleep, the cats frisked here and there in the room, but the sleeper awoke not; they chased each other about the room, and played and romped, and at last they approached Huw's clothes and played with them, and here they seemed to get the greatest amusement, as they turned the clothes about and over, placing their paws now on that string, and now on that button, and ere long their paws were inserted into the pockets of his clothes, and, just as one of the cats had her paw in the pocket that contained Huw Lloyd's purse, he like lightning struck the cat's paw with his sword. With terrible screams they both disappeared, and nothing further was seen of them during the night.

The following morning only one lady was to be seen downstairs at breakfast. Huw was told that the other was slightly indisposed, but he insisted on saying farewell to her as well and was at last taken to her bedside. There he discovered that she had one hand in bandages, and was able on this evidence to rebuke both the sisters and warn them that if they ever dabbled in witchcraft again for their own gain he would make sure that they came to trial.

But the sisters attempted revenge. Soon afterwards Huw left his home to take a service at Festiniog. Glancing back he saw the two witches following him. Immediately he turned round to face them, walking backwards in front of them all the way from Cynvael. He knew that that should he turn his back on them he would be under their power, and that once he reached the porch of the church he was safe. Inside the porch he shouted: 'I defy you now, and before I leave the Church I will make you that you never again witch anyone', and for the rest of their lives they were like other women.

Too many people speed across Anglesey in desperate haste to catch the ferry at Holyhead. After the scenic splendours of Snowdonia this part of their journey may seem an anti-climax, yet the island has much to offer − a beautiful and often lonely coastline, a wealth of historic and prehistoric monuments, and a special feeling that this *is* a place apart, both from the rest of Wales and the rest of Britain.

Anglesey, or Mona as it was then, was the great centre of the Druids. Disciples of that religion came from all over Europe to study on Anglesey, and though much of the teaching was life-giving, Druidism had a darker side as well. Perhaps that is why Anglesey is so rich in the supernatural. Strangely, and at variance with this, Anglesey was also a hotbed for Christianity when the faith arrived in Wales in the sixth century. The first missionaries here were canny in incorporating ancient beliefs within the confines of the new religion. They even adopted the sacred springs of the Druids as their holy wells, and used the carved stonework of pagan structures in new fonts.

The sea features in most of the old stories of Anglesey: the coast is vicious, and was a hazard for ships using the port of Liverpool. In 1743 a farmer, William John Lewis, ploughing his fields with a ploughboy on his farm at Peibio, close to Holyhead, was startled to see a ketch of about 90 tons bearing down on him – *from the sky*. It was sailing about a quarter of a mile above the ground from the direction of the mountains, with its pennants flying and its sails filled. The farmer dashed to the house to fetch his wife, and returned to see the ship return in the direction from which it had come, but now with its sails neatly furled. It was drifting backwards, and the onlookers particularly noticed that a flock of birds mobbed the vessel when it came near them. When questioned more closely about this phenomena, Lewis admitted that he had seen similar ships in the sky before; in fact such events seemed to occur to him at ten-yearly intervals, in much the same way as UFOs are said to return to the same locality every ten years.

Ancient ghosts at modern sites feature in two further hauntings from the west of Anglesey. Roman soldiers are said to have been seen marching around the perimeter of RAF Valley. Hooded monks have also been seen here. When the Wylfa Nuclear Power Station was being constructed in 1964 workmen complained of the ghostly figure of a White Lady who hummed music to them. It seems that the ashes of the opera singer Rosina Buckman were moved when excavations were in progress near the house, Galan Ddu, where she had lived.

The Lligwy Cromlech, near Moelfre, is a particularly fine example of a megalithic tomb. It is also known as Arthur's Quoit, where once a fisherman fell asleep. He dreamed that someone was drowning in the bay just below, crying for help. Waking, and remembering his dream, he dashed to the beach getting there just in time to save a beautiful lady, richly jewelled and dressed all in white. She asked him to carry

Sir John Wynne, adventurer and restless spirit (*National Library of Wales*)

her up to the Great Stone, and there told him that she was, in fact, a witch who had thought it best to disguise herself as a beautiful lady because if he had seen her as an ancient hag, he might have left her to perish. She gave him a small golden ball which she said enclosed a snake-skin charm. He was to keep it secretly, and each year take it down to the shore and immerse it, with the charm inside, in sea-water. If these instructions were carried out good fortune would always follow, but if he lost it, told anyone of it, or took the snakeskin out then his good luck would disappear forever. Whereupon she ran down to the sea, boarded a strange craft, and vanished. For some time all went well. The fisherman followed instructions and prospered. Then a neighbour got to hear of it and stole it. Until the theft was discovered and the ball restored to its rightful owner, all manner of disasters befell the poor man, but after that he kept the ball safely and it was passed down from father to son, even going to India and Australia. Marie Trevelyan says that it was last heard of forty years ago, i.e. in 1860.

Witches came from the sea again at Llanddona, in the north-eastern corner of the island. The legend has it that the Llanddona witches, with their husbands, had been expelled from their native country for practising the black arts, being set adrift in a boat without sails, oars, or rudder. Eventually they came to Llanddona, but the locals, frightened at their appearance, tried to stop them from landing. Then the witches demonstrated their powers by causing a spring of pure water to gush up through the sand, and at this they were allowed on the beach, and there they settled, the men living by smuggling, the women by practising the ancient art. Elias Owen says of them:

It was impossible to overcome these daring smugglers, for in their neckerchief was a fly, which, the moment the knot of their cravats was undone, flew right at the eye of their opponents and blinded them, but before this last remedy was resorted to the men fought like lions, and only when their strength failed them did they release their familiar spirit, the fly, to strike with blindness the defenders of the law.

The women, with dishevelled hair and bared breasts, visited farm houses and requested charity – more as a right than a favour, and no one dared refuse them. If any of the Llanddona Witches made a bid for a pig or anything at fair or market, no one would bid against them, for it was believed they would witch the animal then bought.

The following is one of their curses, uttered at Y Ffynon Oer, a well in the parish, on a man who had offended one of these witches:

Conway Castle

More prosaically, the true reason for Llandonna's reputation as the 'Land of Witches' was the wreck of a Spanish ship in Red Wharf Bay. The survivors were allowed to settle in the neighbourhood and since they were dark in complexion compared with the fair-skinned, fair-haired islanders, and some of them could also perform simple conjuring tricks, they were feared for their supposed powers. No doubt they encouraged the villagers in their fears for some time. The most famous of the Llanddona Witches was Shani Bwt or Little Jane, who at the age of forty was only forty-four inches tall, and had two thumbs on her left hand.

Inland Anglesey is comparatively lean on ghosts, though on one certain night of the year a phantom coach with a liveried driver and four horses is supposed to pass along the road from Llangefni to Penmynydd. It commemorates an incident in which a highwayman held up a mail coach and robbed and killed its passengers. Penmynydd is famous for its dragon. A notable local family was cursed with the prophecy that the Penmynydd dragon would cause the death of the son and heir. Thus the boy was sent abroad and a reward offered to anyone who could kill the beast. A young man of the village successfully tackled it and the corpse of the dragon was displayed for all to admire. The heir returned home, and was taken to view the dead monster, by now practically a skeleton. Scornfully he kicked at the skull, but one of its deadly fangs pierced his shoe, and he died of the poisonous venom, thus fulfilling the prophecy.

Back to the mainland now, and eastwards to the town of Conway nestling beneath the walls of its castle built by Edward I in 1283. When Thomas Pennant visited Conway in the eighteenth century he wrote: 'A more ragged town is scarcely to be seen within; or a more beautiful one without.' Since then many of the higgledy-piggledy Tudor and medieval houses within the town walls which gave rise to his comment have disappeared, making way for larger Victorian buildings, but in spite of this the town manages to retain its haphazard charm today. The finest of the Tudor town-houses in Conway (and probably in all of Wales) is Plas Mawr built by Robert Wynne, third son of Sir John Wynne of Gwydir (who we have met earlier) between 1576 and 1595. Robert Wynne was a wealthy man who increased his fortune by 'adventuring' in the swashbuckling Elizabethan tradition by mixing trade with piracy. Remarkably Plas Mawr remains much as he would have known it, even the extravagant plasterwork surviving intact. Perhaps it is this that gives the house its unique ambience, so that it is easy for visitors to imagine the tragic events that are said to have occurred here nearly three centuries ago.

One of Robert Wynne's successors at Plas Mawr was at one time obliged to leave Conway to fight in a distant war, leaving behind his pregnant wife and young child. At length word came that he was about to return home, and his overjoyed wife climbed to the look-out tower so that she might see his arrival. It was a difficult climb for a woman in the latter stages of pregnancy, especially as she had to help the young child up the steep, narrow steps as well. They remained in the tower for some time, peering at the misty river, until the winter dusk fell. Then they began their descent of the gloomy stairway. Whether it was the mother who missed her footing and fell, dragging the child after her, or the child who slipped and pulled down his mother will never be known. Either way both tumbled to the bottom.

Hearing their screams, the housekeeper hurried to the scene and quickly summoned men to carry the mistress to a bed in the Lantern Room (so called because it held a lantern which lit the courtyard below). The mortally injured child was laid beside her, and a servant sent with a message for the doctor. When, after some time, the servant had not returned with him, another was sent and this time brought a young locum, Doctor Dic, as the senior doctor had already been called out.

Doctor Dic seemed somewhat overwhelmed at having to attend such a high-born patient, but nevertheless examined both the mother and her child, and then called in the housekeeper. Gravely he explained that there was nothing he could do to save them. Both would die. Panic-stricken, and fearing the wrath of the master of the house, the housekeeper fled from the room, locking the door behind her so that the young doctor was imprisoned with the dying woman and her child. Some hours later the master returned to Plas Mawr, and received news of the accident. When the door was unlocked he found his wife and child both dead, but no sign of Doctor Dic, who, it was always assumed, had tried to escape up the wide chimney. Whether he was successful in this was never discovered, for he was never seen in Wales again, so his bones may still rest in some obscure and sooty corner of the chimney. The bereaved husband eventually went mad with grief, and died soon after. His ghost still seeks for the missing doctor in the Lantern Room and, it is said, will continue to do so until he is found, and his remains laid in the churchyard near by.

Conway has a selection of other ghosts – a cloaked figure haunts the ramparts of the castle; the silhouette of a horseman has been seen against the night sky; a bewhiskered sailor, Albert, haunts a house in Berry Street; and a hooded monk walks in the churchyard and along the waterfront.

Clwyd

Llandudno was a small fishing village until the middle years of the last century when its potential as a resort was recognised and it blossomed into the carefully planned town that we see today. At the time of the story of the Gloddaeth Ghost, then, it was a place unknown to tourists, its few inhabitants engaged in farming, fishing, or mining the copper deposits beneath the Great Orme. The district of Gloddaeth is to the east of the town, midway between Penrhyn and Deganwy.

A pest control officer of his day, Thomas Davies of Rhyl was engaged by local farmers to put down foxes which were proving a nuisance to their livestock. He found one fox's den deep in Gloddaeth Wood. Seeing that the cubs were inside with the vixen he settled down to hide amongst the branches of an oak tree that gave a view of the entrance to the den. When the vixen emerged he would be ready to kill her. As he waited he suddenly heard a most blood-curdling and horrible scream that came from the direction of the sea. Then the cry came again, only closer and more anguished. A third time the scream sounded, and by now Davies was certain it was approaching his tree. It was by now getting dark and he was terrified to move in case he should attract the attention of the beast that was calling. Then the terrible cry was repeated, seemingly just below him and he saw the creature that it came from – '. . . a nude being with eyes burning like fire, and these glittering balls were directed towards him. The awful being was a dozen or so yards off. And now it crouched, and now it stood erect, but it never for a single instant withdrew its terrible eyes from the miserable man in the tree, who would have fallen to the ground were it not for the protecting branches.'

Thus poor Davies spent the night in the tree, constantly threatened by the unearthly creature, until as the first hint of dawn lightened the sky the earliest cock crow sounded and at once the beast vanished.

Die (or Dick) Spot you will remember as the wizard who was successful in banishing Cynon's Ghost to ease the making of Lake Vyrnwy. Another story tells how once, on his way to Llanwrst from his home at Denbigh, he called at an inn at Henllan for a pint and a Ploughman's. He was outraged to be charged tenpence for this – sixpence for the bread and cheese, fourpence for the beer. However he paid without comment but before leaving wrote a spell on a piece of paper and stuck it on the underside of a table.

Iolo ap Hugh, prisoner of the enchanted cave (*Welsh Folk Museum*)

At closing time the landlord and his wife went up to bed leaving a maidservant to clear up. But after a while they heard a terrible commotion from the kitchen and when they went to investigate found the girl dancing dementedly, shouting

> *Six and four are ten,*
> *Count it o'er again.*

The landlord angrily shouted at the girl to stop the noise, but this had no effect and when he stepped inside the kitchen he found himself joining in, singing the mad couplet and prancing like a dervish. Moments later the wife too was at it; she entered the kitchen to try to stop the mad dance and was immediately whisked into it. Soon the noise disturbed the neighbours: they guessed the place was bewitched and, knowing that Die Spot had been there earlier, went to fetch him. When he removed the spell from beneath the table the mad dancers were released from the spell. Maybe it's a pity we don't have Die Spot about these days.

Pont-y-Glyn is about six miles west of Corwen on the A5, where the road passes through a twisting ravine. In the bad old days this was a favourite place for highwaymen to lurk, and many travellers were murdered close by. Their ghosts are said to linger here at night especially in the chasm on the Corwen side of the bridge. Here too a man walking home from Corwen late one night was surprised to see a woman sitting dressed in Welsh costume. He said a polite 'good night' to her but she did not reply, and looking back he saw her stand up, whereupon she grew in size like a balloon being inflated until she completely blocked his view of the road.

The famous story of Iolo ap Hugh belongs to Clwyd, though it is impossible to be sure just where the enchanted cave is situated that claimed the fiddle player as its victim.

The entrance to the cave is awesome, and only the foolhardy would approach it closer than they would a volcano, and if they came within five paces of it (as did Iolo) they would inevitably be lost. Branches of its underground passageways extended all over North Wales, one ending inside Chirk Castle. Some said the cavern was the mouth of a hearing trumpet held by the devil himself, so that he could hear what was going on in this upper world without the trouble of a visit. It was a place feared and avoided by beasts as well as by men, and once a fox, pursued by a full pack of hounds, turned to face the hounds rather than seek refuge there. However when the hounds approached they fled from the fox in terror 'such was the smell of assafoetida about him, and his hide was all burnished with green, yellow, and blue lights, as it were with a profusion of will o' the wisps'. Even more miraculous was the conversion of Elias ap Evan, who happened to stagger close to the rim of the forbidden place on the night of a Fair and was 'said to have arrived at home perfectly sober, the only interval of sobriety, morning, noon or night, Elias had been afflicted with for upwards of twenty years.' After this, try as he might, Elias never succeeded in becoming drunk.

Iolo ap Hugh was a merry wandering minstrel, who, one Hallowe'en night (one of the three 'Spirit Nights' which are particularly magical) rashly decided to investigate the cave. He took with him his fiddle, an immense quantity of bread and cheese, and seven pounds of candles. He was never seen again until many years later when an old shepherd who knew Iolo was passing the cave, also on the night of Hallowe'en, and heard wild music coming from the mouth of the cave. And there was Iolo, capering and fiddling madly with a lantern hanging from his chest: 'His face was pale as marble, and his eyes stared fixedly and deathfully, whilst his head dangled loose and unjointed on his shoulders . . . then, he seemed as it were to skate into the cave, quite different from the step of a living and willing man, but he was dragged inwards, like the smoke up a chimney or the mist at sunrise.'

The only monument to Iolo is the wild music that he played. Many years later the old shepherd was attending church one cold winter evening, when a strange burst of music swelled from beneath the aisle – it was Iolo's tune, which was immediately taken down by the organist and is now known as *Ffarwel Ned Pugh*. This tune can also be heard if you visit the cave (if you know where it is and are brave enough) on Hallowe'en night, while on certain nights in a Leap Year there is a star that shines at the far end which enables you to see Iolo and all its other inmates.

The upper reach of the Vale of Llangollen is one of the most lovely parts of Wales, steep pastured hills overlooking the course of the rushing Dee which threads itself between them. The town itself is guarded by the mysterious Dinas Bran, a stronghold that dates from 'that area of time where history and legend merge in an unclear horizon' (Michael Senior, *Portrait of North Wales*). It is a steep climb to reach the ancient fort, but those who do will not solely be rewarded by a magnificent panorama, but may also feel the unique magic of a place that manages to link legendary fable with Christian tradition.

It is also unique in structure, the ancient Celtic ramparts remaining as the basic fortification even as late as the thirteenth century. Its name means Crow, though in Welsh it could also mean Raven, which ties in neatly with an alternative derivation, that this was the fortress of Bran, possibly king of Britain, in about 1060 before the arrival of the Normans. According to the story in the *Mabinogion*, Bran owned a magic cauldron which enabled the dead to be restored to life. Somehow this vessel became confused with the Holy Grail, at the core of Arthurian legend, and it was at the castle of the raven that Sir Launcelot first saw the Grail. In the *Mabinogion* Bran's head is taken to the White Mount in London – and, it was said, as long as it is kept there, within the confines of the Tower of London, this island will be protected against invasion. The fact that another legend says that the ravens which wander about the same grounds are also a magical protection against the same threat seems to give added weight to the Welsh legend.

The story of *The Coalminer who Witnessed his own Funeral* comes from the collection of folk-tales recorded by Robin Gwyndaf. The events took place in the early 1920s.

Well, my father was working now in another coal-mine – in Giatwen between here (Coed-poeth) and Wrecsam. And I worked in the same mine as a youth coming up to twenty years of age, and, as boys do, I would come up from the mine before him and away I would go home, not waiting for him, because he had his partner-in-the-pit to walk home with.

One day I came up from the pit before him and was waiting for him by the pit gate, an unusual thing for me to do. And I walked home with him. After coming three-quarters of the way home there's a big hill coming up from Southsea to the Adwy. And we were talking together, and quite suddenly we stopped talking, and I was in the middle of speaking to him. I looked at him. His face had gone as white as a sheet.

'What's the matter?' I said, 'you aren't ill?'

'Leave me alone', said he, quite sharply.

Well, indeed, I was beginning to think that there was something wrong with him and I asked him again: 'Are you ill?', and he said 'Leave me alone.' And so it was.

Now we walked home in silence up the hill, but when we were within sight of the house he sighed and said:

'Now listen to me! Don't you say anything to your mother!' I was beginning to think that there was something wrong with him then. And so it was.

'Mysterious Dinas Bran'

'Ruthin Castle, haunted by a man in armour' (*National Library of Wales*)

Well now, weeks went by, and I did the same again. I waited for him on top of the pit and walked home with him that day. And by now months had gone by, and in the very same spot where he stopped talking to me first, he said:

'Do you remember the two of us walking up here before, some time ago, and you asked me if I was ill?'

'Yes, indeed, what was the matter with you?'

'Well', he said, 'this is what happened. When we were turning this corner I saw my funeral.'

'Oh! God', I said, and I went into a cold sweat.

And he began to tell the story, the funeral walking up, and he said who the ministers were who walked in front of his coffin. He took some time to tell the story. When we reached the same place in sight of the house he said:

'You take care that you don't tell your mother.'

And so it was. But my blood had turned cold.

However, we changed pits, we went to work in this pit nearer home. He told his partner, Robin Davies, the story, exactly as he told it to me, you see. Well! the strike came in a short while after that. He went to a shop to have his hair cut and was taken ill there. In three or four days my father had died. And his funeral was exactly as he had described it − exactly. And Robin

Davies was in his funeral – he was his partner-in-the-pit at that time. And I saw Robin Davies in two or three days after burying my father, and he could not believe his ears – believe his eyes, isn't it, – so minutely had he described his funeral a few months before his death.

Llandegla is a village between Wrexham and Ruthin. Its Old Rectory was haunted by a very troublesome spirit and a person named Griffiths was called in to lay it. The demon appeared in a variety of forms until at last it became a fly and was trapped in a snuffbox. This was buried under a large stone in the bed of the river close to the bridge near the Mills, and there it was committed to remain until a certain tree grew to reach the parapet of the bridge. As in the case of Lady Jeffrey's spirit, local children took care to keep the top branches cut back.

Ruthin Castle is now a hotel where you may stay and hope to encounter the ghostly figure of a man in armour wearing only one gauntlet. There is also a strange glowing ball of light. George Borrow found the ancient part of the castle very gloomy, and was particularly disturbed by 'that strange memorial of the good old times, a drowning pit' and the whipping-post which stood at the centre of the prison room, or torture chamber.

The village of Llanynys stands on a byway just to the north of Ruthin. Many years ago there was a small house here called Ty Felin. An exciseman on a journey once called at this house late one night to request accommodation. Reluctantly the houseowner showed him to one of the two bedrooms. In the middle of the night he was awoken by some strange sound, and saw standing before him the ethereal shape of a travelling Jew. The exciseman tried to catch him, but having followed him downstairs, lost him in the yard. He returned to his bed, but again and again the shade reappeared, and each time the exciseman left his bed to follow it to the yard. Finally he succeeded in making a mark where the ghost vanished. In the morning he returned to the house with a policeman, and digging below his mark they found a deep well which concealed the body of a wandering Jew. The householder admitted murdering the pedlar some years earlier and was duly brought to the gallows.

Back to the coast now, where Abergele is haunted by the magic ship of Prince Madoc, the *Gwennan Gorn*, in which he is supposed to have discovered America in the twelfth century. The ship was made with nails of staghorn so that Madoc could safely use a lodestone for

navigation, and having sailed from Abergele to Lundy Island (where he picked up his brother) Madoc and the *Gwennan Gorn* vanished for several years. When they returned the ship was manned by a sparse crew. Most had been left to colonise the wonderful land that had been discovered. Madoc gathered together a fleet of ten ships for a further visit to the new land, and it was easy to find volunteers to join him, both men and women, since in the age of violence in which he lived he appears to have been a peace-loving and respected Prince.

Nothing more was heard of this expedition, but in the late eighteenth century an Indian tribe were discovered who were supposed to have understood the Welsh language. These Mandan Indians also had legends and habits which reflected those of ancient Wales: 'Mandan girls were celebrated for their good looks and amiability and were said to be more adept than most. They chattered endlessly even while making love − a fact which one later observer cited as further proof of their Welsh descent!' These lines come from Gwyn Williams's excellent book *Madoc − The Making of a Myth* which is recommended to anyone wishing to pursue the story.

Flint, with the scanty remains of its castle on the shore of the estuary of the Dee, is now at the heart of a rather decayed industrial wasteland.

Centuries ago it was a busy passage port for Ireland, but now it is more of a dormitory for Chester and Liverpool. On its outskirts is Oakenholt, an estate which takes its name from one of the many grand houses that the Victorian tycoons put up in the locality in the last century.

It would seem to be an unlikely place for the appearance of UFOs, yet between 1976 and 1981 one family seems to have enjoyed a peculiar empathy with travellers from another dimension, and their adventures are chronicled in a remarkable book – *Alien Contact: Window on another World*, by Jenny Randles and Paul Whetnall. The entire family were involved in these encounters, but a teenage girl and her younger brother were the main agents of contact, even being taken by the aliens to visit their planet by spacecraft. It is all too easy to dismiss such accounts out of hand: though it is true that when they first attracted publicity, in 1978, the film *Close Encounters of the Third Kind* had just been released. It is also true that children of this age are particularly imaginative, and one unexplained incident could have triggered off others, but there is a weight of cumulative evidence here that cannot be completely dismissed. The Oakenholt aliens were able to penetrate the mind of the girl, and at times it seemed as though she was under their power. Of course the psychic powers of adolescent children are abnormal and are often the cause of the outbreak of poltergeist activity and there may be a link here with her ability to be a mouthpiece of the aliens. Many of the descriptions of the beings themselves, and their spacecraft, etc., confirm accounts from elsewhere which the Flintshire family could not have known about (though they could well have read about the outbreak of UFO activity in Pembrokeshire which took place in the midst of the happenings at Flint).

It is suggested that there are certain windows through which UFOs pass to reach us, and that these may be open in Pembrokeshire and at Flint. And if such events occur today, why should they not have occurred in the past?

Could not the legendary water-horses, which used to whisk people up into the sky and away to distant lands, be a form of space or time travel? Might the Anglesey ship-in-the-sky have been a UFO? Could the fairy people be aliens? After all, our own images of spacecraft are constantly being updated and hardly existed in fiction until fifty years or so ago. Psychic research is taken so seriously today that it seems there is no room for the legends of long ago, but if it is true that Madoc discovered America in 1170, then anything is possible.

Bibliography

Howells, W.	*Cambrian Superstitions*, London, 1831. (Howells was only nineteen when he wrote this book, the source of several of the stories in this one.)
Styles, Showell	*The Mountains of North Wales*, London, 1971.
Trevelyan, Marie	*Folk-Lore and Folk Stories of Wales*, London, 1909. (Although it deals chiefly with South Wales, this book is a most valuable source for legends, stories and customs. Marie Trevelyan was born in 1853 as Emma Mary Thomas, daughter of the mason and stonecarver of Llantwit Major. She was very pretty and in 1880 married a French doctor, but, widowed, she returned to Llantwit in 1898 with her daughter and began collecting folk stories to add to the large collection that she had inherited from her father. She is said to have adopted her bardic name, Marie Trevelyan, as a pen-name. She died in 1922.)
Borrow, George	*Wild Wales*, London, 1869.
Owen, Elias	*Welsh Folk-lore: A Collection of the Folk-tales and Legends of North Wales*, Wrexham, 1896.
Hall, Mr and Mrs S. C.	*The Book of South Wales*, 1861.
Davies, J. Ceredig	*Folk Lore of West and Mid-Wales*.
Masters, Anthony	*The Natural History of the Vampire*.
Clarke, Stephen	*The Ghosts of Monmouth*, 1965.
Halifax, Lord	*Ghost Book*, 1937.
Brown, Roger *(ed.)*	*Turn of the Century Ton*, 1982.
Jones, Glyn and Scurfield, Elfyn	*Sully*, 1986.
Phillips, Martin	*Folklore of Afan and Margam*, 1933.
Simpson, Jacqueline	*British Dragons*, London, 1980.
Jones, T. Gwynn	*Welsh Folklore and Folk Custom*, London, 1930.
Edmunds, George	*The Gower Coast*, Bristol, 1979.
Thomas, Wynford Vaughan	*Portrait of Gower*, 1976 and 1983.
Sikes, Wirt	*British Goblins*, London, 1880.
Pugh, R. J. and Holiday, F. W.	*The Dyfed Enigma*, London, 1979.
Paget, Peter	*The Welsh Triangle*.

Inglis-Jones, E.	*Peacocks in Paradise,* London, 1950.
Coleman, S. J.	*Tales and Traditions of Breconshire,* Douglas, Isle of Man, 1956.
Howse, W. H.	*Radnorshire,* London, 1950.
Arrowsmith, Nancy and Moorse, George	*A Field Guide to the Little People,* London, 1977.
Harris, M. C.	'Legends and Folklore of Llanfachreth Parish', from *Journal of the Merioneth Historical and Record Society,* Vol. 5, 1965.
Jenkins, D. E.	*Bedd Gelert, Its Facts, Fairies, and Folk-lore,* 1899.
Senior, Michael	*Portrait of North Wales,* London, 1957.
Williams, Gwyn	*Madoc – The Making of a Myth,* London, 1979.
Randles, J. and Whetnall, P.	*Alien Contact: Window on another World,* Sudbury, Suffolk, 1981.
Thomas, Wynford Vaughan and Llewellyn, A.	*The Shell Guide to Wales,* London, 1969.